1

The Art of
Everyday Assertiveness:
Speak Up. Say No. Set Boundaries.
Take Back Control.

By Patrick King
Social Interaction Specialist and
Conversation Coach
www.PatrickKingConsulting.com

Table of Contents

Introduction

What does assertiveness mean to you?

I can tell you what it means to me: freedom.

It's not necessarily freedom from others or from the obligations in my life, but assertiveness is the freedom to *choose* what I want to do and not be automatically beholden to people, places, and things.

If it sounds insignificant, it's absolutely not. It's quite analogous to the difference between feeling like you're drowning versus treading water effortlessly. And if it sounds familiar, then welcome to taking back your time, energy, and life.

I'm a recovering people-pleaser, passive person, and overall doormat. I realize now that I acted in this manner for a few reasons. First, I didn't know that it was okay to say no to people. Second, I felt like people would hate me if I disagreed with them. Third, I literally didn't know the words to use. These sound almost silly to read back as I write them, but I know I'm not alone in them.

I wrote this book as much for me as for you. To freedom!

Chapter 1. The Balance of Assertiveness

It takes more than communication skills to navigate the minefield of interpersonal and working relationships.

What if you still find yourself going to extreme lengths to avoid conflict, unable to express yourself clearly and fairly without your emotions sabotaging you? What if you beat yourself up for being such a pushover, losing your temper, or following orders against your better nature?

Assertiveness is, in theory, easy as saying some simple phrases. But in practice, it's one of the most difficult parts of human interaction and often a fine line to walk. In order to change this behavior, you must first be able to recognize it in yourself and others.

Three friends had been meaning to meet up so Keisha booked a table for dinner that night. She ordered the most expensive meal because her promotion allowed her to treat herself. Michael hadn't told them he was recovering from gastric flu and didn't order food, excusing himself, sweating and shaking, to throw up halfway through the meal.

Gita had paid out for unexpected car repairs that day and, hiding a gasp when she saw the prices, just ordered a side dish so she could afford a much-needed drink.

When the bill came, Keisha told the waiter they would split it three ways.

Michael resented paying for their food when he should have been at home in bed, but he agreed, not wanting to disappoint Keisha. Gita, probably helped along by the house wine on an almost empty stomach, snapped that Keisha was too controlling and they should have cancelled.

"Why didn't you both just *say*?" Keisha asked as she theatrically paid for the entire meal amidst protests that turned into deafening silence. That was the last time they met up as friends.

Most people can remember a time when they have played the role of Keisha, Gita, or Michael. Assertiveness would have been a very welcome guest at their dinner table for all three parties.

Michael's passive behavior stemmed from feeling too guilty to tell Keisha he wasn't well enough to meet up. Gita was ashamed of her financial situation, which bubbled into mistrust of Keisha's intentions. Despite Keisha's outward appearance, her low self-worth fueled her aggressive behavior surrounding where, when, and how they ate together.

What is assertiveness and why does it matter?

Assertiveness allows you to let people know where you stand without negativity attaching itself to your choices. It's how you are able to extract what you want, without the negative consequences. Think of assertiveness as a bubble protecting your values, availability, capability, and needs—your confident bodyguard who stops things from spiraling out of control. It doesn't allow you to overstretch yourself or fear imposing on other people. Being assertive is calmly standing up for your rights and respectfully influencing others in potentially stressful situations.

Assertiveness improves interactions with colleagues, family, friends, and strangers in all circumstances. It can achieve great outcomes as a result of doing things you prefer to avoid, like making a complaint or asking for a pay raise. You may find yourself on the receiving end of benefits you wouldn't have dreamed of before you started practicing assertiveness.

Asserting Your Needs

We all have needs, psychological or physical, and the inability to be assertive means your needs go unfulfilled. On a short-term basis, this is acceptable and sometimes even necessary. But is that how you want to live your life—a state of deprivation and lacking?

Needs are a big part of who you are: they become the indulgent daydreams of your deepest desires, what you wish for when you toss a coin into a fountain or see a shooting star, or the goals you enter into your app or journal on New Year's Day. They are everybody's driving force, and unmet needs create feelings of anxiety, hopelessness, and unhappiness.

It's important to understand the needs that you have to meet, as they are what you've been missing out on by not being assertive. This is what you're giving up in life—the costs—by always letting things slide and not speaking up for yourself. Noted personal development speaker and author Tony Robbins defined the following universal six core human needs.

(1) Certainty is the need for consistency, stability, security, safety, order, comfort, and control. It is a basic need that focuses on survival and the ability to build a structure and a routine in safe conditions.

Without assertiveness: If your housemate failed to spend the money you gave him on paying rent and bills and you didn't confront him, leading to angry letters from the landlord and your water and electricity being cut off, this need would not be met.

However, human beings are complex creatures; too much **certainty** leads to boredom. This is where **(2) variety** comes in: this is the need for diversity, challenge, change, surprise, uncertainty, and adventure.

Without assertiveness: Your housemate always pays his way but views redecorating as a waste of time. Your décor gets you down but you can't find it in you to convince him a makeover is the right move. You almost wish he'd stop paying the rent; then at least you could find somewhere new.

(3) Significance is the need to feel needed, honored, wanted, special, and validated. From birth, we need to feel unique and worthy of attention, and one way we can achieve the feeling of **significance** is through teaching.

Without assertiveness: A teaching position you'd love to have is being advertised at work. It's assumed your outgoing colleague will get the role, but they're not really interested and you know you'd be great. You can't quite bring yourself to make your case to the hiring manager, though, and they eventually give the job to a less qualified candidate.

(4) Love and connection is the need for communication, connection, intimacy, and shared love with others.

Without assertiveness: Despite months of hints, you couldn't bring yourself to take the plunge and ask someone who cared for you deeply on a date. The moment was there, but you faltered and they left, sadness ingrained on their face. A few months later, you found out from a friend that they had a new partner now. **Significance** only goes so far, as humans crave a much deeper connection.

(5) Growth is the need for intellectual, spiritual, physical, and emotional development. This need takes you from matters of the personality to matters of the spirit. Without the previous needs taken care of, you can't begin to grow.

Without assertiveness: Your company is offering training in public speaking, but when signing people up, they laugh and walk past you, joking that the timid mouse wouldn't dare. You stare silently at their backs as they walk off and resign yourself to the fact that people like you don't deserve to conquer their fears.

Finally, **(6) contribution** is the need to do good, serve others, give, protect beyond ourselves, and provide care.

Without assertiveness: You've always dreamed of rescuing animals but you're scared of convincing the shelter staff; you suppose the animals would be better off elsewhere and block out thoughts of the lives you could improve. Your attempts at veganism stop when your friends laugh that you wouldn't last a week. You eat the meat they cooked and tell them you were only joking.

The examples above illustrate how fulfilling your six core human needs will necessarily involve interacting with other people. Being assertive with them would have prevented the outcomes outlined above; you could have had your newly decorated apartment, dream teaching job, a partner, and a pet.

Even if throughout your life your needs haven't been met, you still have them, just like everyone else. It will be impossible to behave assertively if you tell yourself you don't have needs but resent others who you feel demand too much and never think of your best interests.

You will need to work with the people in your life to fulfill your needs and, for the first time ever, perhaps, discover balance.

Balance

We've just taken a quick look at the worst-case scenarios. You understand that if you lack assertiveness, it's easy to repress or be overwhelmed by your natural needs. You're ready to believe that you deserve to be fulfilled, and you might have come into this book ready to crack some skulls.

So where does balance come in? Other people have needs, too.

Although it's important to focus on yourself, it's all too easy to go from one extreme to the other. If you feel people have stood in the way of your needs, an obvious emotional response will be anger, maybe even the desire for revenge. You may begin to feel you are owed something and blame others for the fact you're insecure or aren't achieving what you want. Assertiveness isn't about selfishly denying others their needs so yours can be met.

You'll never be able to stop other people asking something of you, but you always have the power to say no. People will behave however they want, and they, too, may repress or inflate their needs because of their past experiences. Just wishing that they wouldn't isn't being assertive. Being assertive is understanding that you can't control what others may do, but you can control your own behavior.

For example, take control of your personal space, but in a respectful way. Don't allow people to push ahead of you in queues, but at the same time, don't block walkways or push in yourself. You have the right to physically defend yourself if necessary, but there is no need to be a physical threat to others. This is balance.

Another example is boundaries. Boundaries are important for security and maintaining feelings of self-worth. It is in your best interest to tell anyone you have any relationship with if something makes you uncomfortable, but you can't let this develop into constant criticism of how they aren't meeting your needs and actually go on the attack. You can set boundaries by striving to always say no in a healthy way. Never refusing anything puts you at the whim of others, but using the threat of a no to manipulate other people doesn't allow them to nourish healthy boundaries either. This is also balance.

Balancing your own needs with those of the people around you is an important part of being assertive.

Sometimes It Pays to Not Be Nice

You may have witnessed people who seem to always get what they want despite not acting in a balanced way. You may even have your own bad habits that you continue to fall back on, such as bullying people into saying yes or ignoring a request until it goes away. It can't be denied that such tactics may help you achieve some of your six core human needs, though they may not help you to reach the levels of **love and connection**, **growth**, and **contribution**. But do we have better outcomes overall if we're a little selfish to the point of neglecting balance?

In the study "Aggression, Exclusivity, and Status Attainment in Interpersonal Networks" published in the journal *Social Forces*, sociologist Robert Faris followed students in grades six to eight from three North Carolina counties for three years.

Faris used factors like being voted "most likely to succeed" in yearbooks to determine the "elite" students and then looked at who they had named as their friends. The "hangers-on" had named a member of the elite as their friend but hadn't been named back. Students also shared who they'd treated badly and who had been cruel to them.

The elite represented only 5% of all the schools, with their friends and hangers-on totaling 14%. Faris found that the last 81% of students were still able enter the top tier through "reputational aggression," which included gossiping, shunning, spreading rumors, and teasing.

This behavior doubled the chances of becoming friends with one of the elite, particularly if the aggressive behavior was targeted at a high-status student or their close friends. The victims of reputational aggression slunk down to the depths of the second or third tier of the hierarchy.

Assertive behavior is neither passive nor aggressive. People wishing to become more assertive may worry that they'll be considered "not nice." The reality is that being assertive will involve you refusing things that aren't right for you. Most people don't like to be turned down, but it's how you handle the refusal that determines how others perceive you.

Passive people don't reach their goals—in this case, popularity—and may not even be aware that it's what they want. They would likely have been part of the 81% not targeted, or if they were part of the elite to begin with, they would have failed to stand up to the aggression.

Aggressive people made it to the elite by targeting other students. This got them what they wanted, but they had to use unhealthy behaviors and ultimately put themselves in the firing line for other aggressive people to target them, following their example. It did pay for the aggressive people to not be nice. They achieved **significance** but gambled with **certainty**, **love and connection**, and **growth**.

An assertive student at one of the three schools studied may have desired popularity but chose to join clubs, attend social events, and demonstrate strengths like loyalty and kindness to achieve this. Assertive behavior would lead to healthier relationships, and although they could be targeted by an aggressive person wishing to join the elite, they would likely stand up for themselves in a way that commanded respect. In other words, there are inevitable consequences for aggression.

To meet your own needs, it's important to remember that you have the choice to be aggressive, passive, or assertive. Passivity is what we must move away from and likely the reason you're reading this in the first place. Aggressiveness is actually helpful in small doses, but not for long-term fulfillment. Assertiveness is the overall goal because of its balance.

Like all art forms, assertiveness takes practice. Without the solid foundations required to build an assertive personality, self-doubt and anxiety cloud your ability to make respectful, objective decisions for yourself. If you don't understand the limitations set on you by your experiences of having your needs met, you will continue to be aggressive, passive, or feel shame like Keisha, Michael, and Gita.

Robbins's six core human needs introduced you to the universal needs that everyone is trying to meet. The students willing to use reputational aggression for a taste of popularity show how tempting it can be to act selfishly and without balance. However, this type of behavior doesn't achieve the healthy outcomes you earn by practicing assertiveness.

Assertiveness is asking for what you want, turning others down, and making decisions that are right for you without anger, threats, manipulation, or fear of repercussions. Everybody deserves to have their needs met while maintaining their sense of self-worth, and no matter what others may do, you always have the power to control how you react.

Takeaways:

1. Assertiveness requires a delicate balance, especially if you are new to it. You may have started as too passive, but take care to not swing into the aggressive territory where you are robbing other people of their assertiveness. Aggressiveness does pay off in small ways, but there is often a long-term toll to pay.

2. Tony Robbins succinctly articulated the six needs of human happiness you are likely keeping yourself from as a result of lacking assertiveness. They are **certainty**, **variety**, **significance**, **love and connection**, **growth**, and **contribution**.

Chapter 2. "Just Let It Go."

While children throughout the world regularly belt the theme song from the Disney movie *Frozen* and encourage everyone to "let it go" when it comes to being taken advantage of over and over, letting it go and pretending the treatment will disappear on its own rarely helps the situation. Whether it is an innate need to please others, a strong desire to avoid conflict at all costs, or a misguided attempt to do the right thing, people who avoid being assertive often find themselves the victim in certain relationships and are desperately looking for a way out.

While compromise, working together, and making sacrifices in various relationships are not faulty character traits, there are those who will take advantage of a peacekeeper's good nature, thus making the peacekeeper feel disregarded, disrespected, and devalued. Does this sound familiar?

This chapter will explore some of the motivation behind the dynamics of both you, who wishes to be more assertive, and those who would seek to keep you down. It also offers advice about how to avoid becoming a victim.

Sacrifice vs. Suffering

Living a sacrificial lifestyle is not in and of itself a bad thing. Some of the most admired people of history were willing to make sacrifices for the betterment of mankind. Marin Luther King Jr., Gandhi, John F. Kennedy, and Rosa Parks were all people who committed great acts of sacrifice during their lifetimes. A willingness to live a life that allows the needs of others to become a priority, however, does not mean a constant denial of your own needs. In other words, sacrifice does not have to equal suffering—something of a common theme when learning assertiveness.

It should be noted, therefore, that people who do not assert themselves in certain situations can become victims of those who always look out for their own interests, no matter how it affects others. When one individual allows another to win all the time, whether that's choosing how much money to spend on a car, pushing forward a particular proposal at work, or dictating the daily schedule, the other person will feel like a loser in all these battles, and resentment, anger, and frustration will increase.

Emotional Blackmail

Emotional blackmail is the dynamic that most frequently occurs to make you lack assertiveness and otherwise let things slide when you *really* shouldn't. Conventional blackmail occurs when one person tries to force another to do something by holding some sort of threat over the victim. We are all familiar with the plot wherein the corrupt politician votes for big tobacco because he does not want the compromising photographs of him and his mistress to reach his wife's hands.

Emotional blackmail, which can happen at work, in families, or among friends, was first coined by Susan Forward in 1998, and it often goes far beyond a physical threat and causes the victim to comply out of a sense of guilt, fear, or obligation. It is possible that the victim builds up the threat in his or her head, but real or not, people who are the victim of emotional blackmail find themselves complying with the desires of the blackmailer by remaining quiet and avoiding confrontation.

Forward articulated four main types of emotional blackmail you may or may not be familiar with.

The **punisher's threat** occurs when the victim receives this message from the perpetrator: "Do what I want, or you will suffer negative consequences." While the above example of the unscrupulous politician fits this, many other experiences do as well. At work, a victim might feel like her ideas will be criticized in front of the boss if she does not agree with the strategic plan of her team. At home, one partner might feel as if the other will withhold physical intimacy if certain expectations are not met. Even if the threat is not spoken, the victim believes the negative consequence will happen if he or she does not go along.

The **self-punisher's threat** takes advantage of the victim's sense of guilt by sending the message "Do what I want, or I will make myself suffer negative consequences." Often this scenario includes high drama. For example, in a dating relationship, one person might threaten self-harm if the other person does not want to continue the relationship. A child might hold his breath until his mom gives in and buys the candy bar at the market checkout. If this sort of manipulation seems childish and immature, it is. People utilizing this technique to get their way are desperate to control relationships and are not above resorting to drastic measures.

Closely related to the self-punisher's threat is the **sufferer's threat**. Rather than the threat of self-harm, the manipulator in this situation says, "Do what I want, or *I* will suffer negative consequences from the outside." A classic example of this sort of threat can be seen when a friend begs another friend not to rat him out. Consider Terry and Tracy. Terry has a car accident while driving under the influence and destroys Tracy's neighbor's mailbox. Tracy wants to confess the incident to the neighbor so the damage is repaired. Terry, however, convinces Tracy to keep quiet about the incident because it could lead to his arrest, prosecution, and incarceration for drunk driving. Terry could even twist this to the point that Tracy would feel responsible for Terry's revoked driver's license, even though Tracy was not in the car and was not drinking the night of the incident. The manipulator in this situation manipulates the blame so that he becomes the victim while the true victim of the emotional blackmail is made to feel like the bad guy in the situation.

The final form of emotional blackmail is identified as the **tantalizer's threat**. Opposite of the other three threats, this one holds the possibility of a reward coming to the victim. Rather than threatening a negative consequence, the perpetrator sends the message "Do what I want, and you will possibly enjoy positive consequences." While the use of a reward system is often very effective in behavior modification methodology, it can be used quite harshly in adult relationships. Take for example, a manager who indicates that a subordinate in the accounting department should approve a questionable expenditure while hinting that the company will allow the accountant to make similar expenditure claims in the future. The accountant may not want to break company policy, but under the direction of a supervisor and with the implied promise of future personal financial gain, the accountant may feel pressured into bending the rules even if he personally finds it unethical.

FOG

While it may be easy to look at these emotional blackmail threats as too obvious and easy to avoid, the underlying fact remains that most of us are still driven by remarkably similar emotions that lead to a lack of assertiveness.

You may or may not be driven by emotional blackmail, or you might be driven by what Forward identifies as three major components in fear, obligation, and guilt (FOG) that drive targets of emotional blackmail to fall into patterns wherein they remain on the down side of an imbalance of power.

Let's begin with fear.

It is one of the most basic instincts. Survival often depends on the response to fear. A victim of emotional blackmail fears negative consequences and the missed opportunity for reward. Just like fear drives a kitten to hide from an active toddler, fear will drive a person to comply with a blackmailer. The kitten may be avoiding physical discomfort or harm while the victim is avoiding confrontation and the potential for an unpleasant outcome.

Many people are excellent at imagining the worst-case scenario in every situation, but rarely does the worst-case scenario become reality. When sending a child to summer camp, some parents imagine the worst thing that could possibly happen. They visualize their child dead in the lake after being chopped up by the blades of a motor boat. While tragedies do occur, most children at summer camp enjoy the lake and come home with nothing more than a sunburn, mosquito bites, and a treasure trove of happy memories.

Second, many victims feel obligated to their blackmailer. Perhaps it is because they feel a sense of loyalty or the need to repay for past considerations or favors. The blackmailer may even be a scorekeeper who regularly reminds the victim of his or her indebtedness. The victim feels the need to go along. There is a sense of duty, whether real or imagined.

Finally, guilt can be a factor in causing people to follow the directions of the empowered one in the relationship. In reality, guilt is actually a natural emotion that serves a real purpose. It provides an inner signal that an action will harm another. When the feeling is appropriate, guilt protects or helps mend relationships when something hurtful happens. The problem with guilt is that it often appears without appropriate cause.

In his classic book on recovery, *Healing the Shame That Binds You (1988)*, John Bradshaw explains the difference between guilt and shame. "Guilt says I've done something wrong; shame says there is something wrong with me. Guilt says I've made a mistake; shame says I am a mistake. Guilt says what I did was not good; shame says I am no good." Like guilt, not all shame is bad, in fact experiencing shame is a natural part of growing up and helps develop a sense of humility. Toxic shame, however, can prevent people from taking a stand for themselves.

It is often difficult to separate whether the cause of the imbalance within the relationship is fear, obligation, or guilt. In fact, most often, it is actually a combination of the three that creates a desire to comply without question. When a person fears for their position within a relationship, feels an obligation toward the more powerful person in the relationship, and experiences guilt about potential damage to the relationship, the combination reinforces the desire to go along even when feeling overwhelmed and undervalued. Your worst nightmare *could* happen, but it is highly unlikely to.

The key to avoiding victimization is taking time to reflect on personal reactions to various situations and learning to recognize feelings of fear, obligation, and guilt. By recognizing patterns and reactions, victims can begin to gain more control and restore balance in their relationships. Confrontation, which is often the one thing victims want to avoid most, is inevitable. Victims will have to confront their own fears, senses of obligation, and feelings of guilt. Likewise, they are going to have to confront the blackmailer. While these are daunting tasks, victims must assert themselves in order to break the cycle.

Just like real fog makes late-night driving difficult, FOG can make people feel paralyzed and powerless in some relationships. Finding the correct path may seem next to impossible. It is conceivable, however, to take control and conquer fear, obligation, and guilt and become more assertive.

Many of life's greatest achievements are realized when fears are faced and overcome. The thought of riding a roller coaster sends many pre-adolescents scrambling for excuses as to why they cannot, but the exhilaration of the first dip ignites a desire for more that are bigger, higher, and faster. Being responsible for the life of another human being is terrifying, yet most parents would say it is well worth it.

Self-advocacy in a relationship that is out of balance can be intimidating; it can spark fears and cause anxiety; yet if the end result produces a more balanced and healthy relationship, the risk outweighs the fear of the potential conflict—at least, in theory. Reality might play out a little differently.

Additional Factors That Hamper Assertiveness

The components of FOG have a tremendous effect on a person's ability to be more assertive in various relationships. Fear, obligation, and guilt—turned to shame and perhaps even anger—hamper confidence and fuel self-doubt. There are, however other factors that contribute to a person refusing to be assertive. It is important to note that these characteristics are not necessarily character flaws, but when manifested in the extreme, they can cause a person to feel devalued and unworthy of being in healthy, well-balanced relationships.

Have you ever called yourself a perfectionist? The perfectionist is constantly seeking approval from others through actions. By being flawless or blameless, no one else has room to say anything negative. This gives you value and immunity from rejection. However, perfectionists are often fearful that when they question a decision or refuse to go along, they will no longer have any value within the relationship.

Equally at risk are those with low self-esteem or a low sense of self-worth. Not only do they devalue themselves, they also put the other person on a pedestal, believing the other person's happiness is more important than their own. Harboring an unfounded fear that rejection of a request will be viewed as a rejection of the person, victims avoid confrontation in hopes of preserving the relationship.

Finally, some people avoid asserting themselves because they do not want to close doors they feel they will need open in the future. If saying no or asserting their own desires is perceived as reason for ending a relationship, then perhaps it is a relationship that needs to be ended. Maintaining an unbalanced relationship can cause stress, sleeplessness, and chaos, which are far more damaging than actually ending the relationship.

Learning to Assert

So how do people fix relationships based on a toxic imbalance of power? Obviously, ignoring the issue, hoping it will change on its own, or pretending it is not really a problem allows people to continue the status quo with no disruption to the proverbial apple cart. Yet those reactions will undoubtedly lead to dissatisfaction, resentment, and eventual deterioration of the victim's sense of self-value and the overall fulfillment within relationship.

Becoming assertive requires action and practice.

There is no way around it, even if it feels uncomfortable. Naturally, victims will experience fear the first time they try to take a stand, but just as a child must conquer the fear of crossing the threshold of a kindergarten classroom in order to grow intellectually, victims must conquer their fears about confrontation. Fear and doubt are expected responses, but remember that fear often helps people identify areas for growth while doubt kills more dreams than failure or rejection ever will.

After an assertive act, a person is likely to feel guilt, perhaps even shame. These responses should become less strong as a person has more practice with self-assertion and realizes how good it can feel to have his or her needs met. Victims of emotional blackmail do not need to remain victims forever.

The process of becoming comfortable with assertiveness is not a quick fix. Remember that FOG is never based on reality. The worst fears rarely materialize, obligations are often perceived, and guilt is almost always self-inflicted. Being patient and persistent while learning assertiveness will pay off in most relationships, but if the elements of your FOG are truly realistic, that's a sign of larger problems.

Some people, however, really struggle with some aspects of becoming more assertive. Continuous feelings of guilt and shame can become overwhelming. Untying the emotional knots of years of experiencing self-doubt, guilt, shame, fear, and unworthiness can be a difficult process. Based on the World Values Survey and a set of clinical experiments, Andrew Vonasch concluded that most people are willing to experience extreme physical discomfort in order to avoid having their reputations damaged. Thus, is it better to be a pushover or doormat than to risk damaging your reputation?

Preserving a reputation as someone who is nice, generous, or likeable might cause a person to think twice before attempting to be assertive. On the other hand, people who want mature, healthy relationships must be willing to compromise and work together. They must avoid scorekeeping and invalidating the other's feelings; they must work to meet needs that arise within relationships.

Will there be some who do not respond well to assertion and never learn to play nice? Absolutely. Consider two friends who regularly meet for dinner. Grace always arrives on time, while Jane is always at least 20 minutes late. For years, Grace has ignored her friend's tardiness, but one day she decides to tell Jane how uncomfortable it makes her to wait alone, sipping a glass of wine and wondering whether or not Jane will arrive.

Jane essentially has two possible responses to Grace's assertion. The dynamic has suddenly been changed, and Jane can either recognize Grace's feelings and make an effort to be more prompt or she can minimize Grace's feelings and continue to arrive late.

Hopefully, Jane will choose the mature, healthy response and try to help Grace feel like she is valued in the relationship by meeting on time. If, however, she does not, then Grace still has control; she can make a decision whether or not this friendship, which occasionally feels disrespectful and unkind, is worth preserving. Suddenly, Grace, who has been passive on this issue, has power. No matter what happens between the two of them, by asserting herself and making her desires known, Grace automatically changes the balance of power.

In the end, becoming more assertive in various relationships is not about determining who holds power or who is the blackmailer and who is the victim; it is really about everyone in the relationship feeling valued and having their needs met. By taking steps to become more assertive, people have the opportunity to improve many different relationships.

Takeaways:

1. Too often, we feel like we must "let things go" for one reason or another. Are these reasons real or imagined? Important or irrelevant? Sometimes they appear important because of emotional blackmail, which is when there is an implicit threat that causes people to not assert themselves. There are four specific types of emotional blackmail threats: punisher, self-punisher, sufferer, and tantalizer.

2. Even if there don't appear to be forms of emotional blackmail, the elements of FOG—fear, obligation, and guilt—will make you avoid speaking up.

3. Other causes for "letting it go" include perfectionism and low self-esteem. The best way to learn to assert, as uncomfortable as it sounds, is consistent action and practice. Take baby steps at first, and the tension will begin to subside each time. You can find more about this in the assertiveness action plan in Chapter 9.

Chapter 3. Nobody Else Will Put You First

Here's a hard truth in life: even those you rely on for support and love, like your birth family or chosen family, will never be able to care about you like you should care about yourself.

You're entirely responsible for your own happiness and destiny. This might be daunting for some who let others affect their choices, satisfaction, and even whether or not today will be a good day, but it actually puts you in a position of strength. If you put the hard work in and strategically plan the life you want, it's in your hands to achieve it. Assertiveness is the only way to guarantee that someone in the world has your best interests at heart. Putting yourself first and liking yourself enough to ask for what you need means that even when you feel alone there is always one person you can depend on—you.

Self-Prioritization

The first step in this process is to prioritize yourself.

It's instilled in many people from a very young age that putting others first makes you a good person. Altruism, the principle of being charitable and selfless, has been proven to benefit physical and mental well-being; you may have heard of people with depression being encouraged to volunteer and help others in need to lessen their focus on their own pain.

However, any potential benefits to altruism are lost when you prioritize other people's needs before your own. If you were taught that it was positive to push yourself to the limit, be productive, and give your all to help others, it's easy to take this to extreme levels. You end up ignoring your own needs and making sacrifices and decisions that hold you back. This not only hurts you but negatively impacts the people you think you're helping.

Altruism in a balanced lifestyle where prioritizing yourself is a good thing, but when your life is entirely devoted to looking after others, it stops you from being assertive. It isn't balanced or healthy to believe that your primary role in life is to serve others. Sometimes it's necessary to cast altruism aside and stop putting others first and focus more generally on prioritizing yourself, your desires, and your needs.

Consider the parents who praise their child for letting a friend play with his toys without a fuss. They overlook the fact that his friend snatches the toys and pushes their son when he tries to share. Despite his own discomfort and the unfairness of it all, their child learns that accepting this unfair treatment makes him a "good boy." His altruistic behavior is being reinforced, and his understanding of the world is that total sacrifice is needed to make others happy.

This would have been a perfect scenario for the parents to teach their child about assertiveness. Instead, his needs are overshadowed by his parents' desire for the children to get along and for them to have a kind, giving son. This is just as unfair as the friend's desire to be in charge overshadowing the child's need to feel equal and safe.

Often people stifle their own *needs* to satisfy someone else who is actually only expressing a small *desire*. Desires are unnecessary cravings that come from what you want, such as being rich enough to have a private jet. Needs are what humans must have in order to survive, such as the need to receive a wage that is enough for you to afford food, water, and shelter. It's unbalanced for you to prioritize what other people might want versus what you truly need. Needs can't be met without assertiveness.

For many, life is a movie—at best a glitzy rom-com or at worst a horror—where they're the lead character. They see themselves as the heroes, with everyone else in their life acting as less important minor characters. If you agree that others are the lead characters and you serve as their sidekick, you may be suffering from "supporting actor syndrome." This prevents you from ever prioritizing yourself.

Selfless behaviors from "supporting actor syndrome" negatively affect your life. You might have stayed up late consoling your friend who broke up with their partner only to sleep through your alarm and wake to a text from them telling you they're back together and so glad they don't have work that day. This is likely one of many examples where their needs come first in your relationship with them.

Some friends will disappear once they realize you can no longer be their supporting actor. You slowly spent your savings and put your own life on hold to help someone get back on their feet who promptly dropped you once they realized what they thought was an endless supply of patience and money was drying up. You see serving and prioritizing others as your role because you don't see yourself as the hero in your own movie, and you always lose out because of this.

You may argue that you do prioritize yourself, but only once you've done your "good deeds," because doing these things makes you a nice person.

Perhaps you have a schedule full of favors for others but always plan and look forward to some you-time on Saturdays. Only, last Saturday you had to drive your friend to the airport because she doesn't trust taxis to be on time; the one before that, you had to work to help out a colleague who was behind on a project; the one before that, you ended up grocery shopping for your neighbor whose check hadn't cleared . . .

Telling yourself that *after* you've sorted out your to-do list you'll prioritize yourself is useless. It's also a contradiction. The time you assume you'll have just doesn't exist. Instead of making room to help others, you should always prioritize yourself.

Schedule the time dedicated to your needs for when you can be at your most relaxed and focused. If you can only prioritize yourself for short, hurried bursts between multitasking, it's unlikely anything you do will be relaxing, rejuvenating, or the start of a new healthy habit. The online course you purchased will stay unstudied if you're a morning person attempting to read the textbook at 1:00 a.m. after a long day working, raising the children, or both.

Whether you're a night owl or full of energy at the crack of dawn, the time when you're the most productive needs to be prioritized and uninterrupted. If you schedule a yoga session before work, then assert that you're unavailable for that half hour, no matter how much someone at work "needs" you to grab coffees on the way in.

Self-Compassion

The word compassion means "to suffer with," and self-compassion is when you accept your own suffering and show yourself love, empathy, and acceptance, particularly in the face of failure. Basically, it's when you're kind to yourself and put your feelings and care above those of others.

You may think that helping others is a path to happiness, but the problem is that your list of things you "should" be doing to ease others' suffering is overwhelming and endless, from volunteering at a local charity to keeping in touch with old friends to trying to please your boss, partner, landlord, strangers . . .

Ignoring or ridiculing your own suffering and choosing instead to try and ease everyone else's is unhealthy. Despite your guilt and the hope that helping all these external people and causes will make you feel better, research has shown that practicing self-compassion actually improves your own well-being. This in turn benefits those around you.

Researcher Kristin Neff defined three important behaviors in self-compassion.

First, treating yourself kindly lets you look at your mistakes from a view of sympathy and concern; it provides the safety needed to actually learn from your mistakes and make true changes. Second, practicing mindfulness through observing your thoughts and feelings as they happen, accepting rather than becoming consumed by them. Lastly, developing a sense of common humanity prevents you feeling isolated from others or somehow separate in your battles.

If you practice self-compassion, you will be kinder to yourself, more comfortable in your own skin, and understanding of the struggles others are facing in theirs.

The enemy of self-compassion is self-criticism. It's likely you haven't given much thought to the way you talk to yourself. Your internal dialogue goes largely unmonitored and isn't impartial.

It's important to start listening to your inner voice and notice how often what you're saying is negative, defeatist, and cruel. You would never speak to a friend how you speak to yourself. Even if there was an element of truth to the point your internal dialogue's trying to make, you'd phrase it in a helpful and kind way if you were talking to someone you cared about.

There will always be opportunities for you to practice self-compassion. Imagine (or perhaps remember) a time where you didn't prepare properly and are now running late for an important appointment. The next train is delayed and you're flustered and furious at yourself. There are two ways you can handle this. You can fall into old habits or remember that the assertive way of life is about self-preservation and satisfaction.

The first is *without* self-compassion. Your disappointment turns to anger and your thoughts spiral into all the other times you've been late, how you never learn, and how stupid you are. You give up and go home, where you ignore your phone when it rings. Your bad mood spills over into the rest of the day and you pick a fight with someone you care about before indulging in a bad habit you've tried to break.

The second is *with* self-compassion. You remember Kristin Neff's advice and practice mindfulness, acknowledge common humanity, and respond to yourself kindly. You want to alleviate your suffering so you admit that it doesn't make you a terrible person for running late, and even though it is your fault, you choose not to punish yourself. Think of the kindness and reassurance you would offer a friend in this situation and extend that compassion to yourself. It's okay, and it doesn't make you a bad person.

You've conditioned yourself to believe negative things about who you are, and each time you hurt yourself in this way, you're reinforcing the idea that you're undeserving of kindness, from yourself and others. The truth is, you deserve much better—an internal voice that isn't your worst critic but your best friend and cheerleader.

Self-Acceptance

If other people aren't going to put your needs first, they're certainly not going to be there to give you around-the-clock reassurance and validation. They can't cure your insecurities or self-doubts, nor will the superficial "improvements" you make to please others be able to fix the suffering you feel inside.

Resenting or loathing any part of yourself will always hold you back. Refusing to resist any part of who you are is vital to establishing your needs and getting them met, even if you do choose to live an unconventional lifestyle or ignore your hairdresser's advice to color your gray hairs.

Self-acceptance is accepting that everything that's happened in your life has led you to be who you are and act how you do, and you're doing your best based on your experiences, knowledge, and situation. The relationship you have with yourself sets the scene for every relationship you will ever have. If you believe that, despite your flaws, you have the right to do what is best for you, you will behave assertively.

Dr. Robert Holden said, "No amount of self-improvement can make up for any lack of self-acceptance." Holden found that trying to improve how he appeared to others took him further away from what could make him truly happy inside.

Treating himself with compassion and kindness in all his "messy glory" and being willing to love himself stopped him seeking external gratification. He was able to find love within and forgive himself for letting his need to be different prevent him from feeling joy. Holden said that you must "understand that the only reason you need to forgive is to restore yourself to the authentically happy person you are here to be."

A talented actor wins a scholarship to a prestigious drama school but finds that everyone there is younger, wealthier, and has industry connections. Despite rave reviews, she never feels like she belongs and stops auditioning for parts, convinced the casting agents just pity her.

Self-acceptance would have allowed her to see that although there were advantages the others had that she didn't, she was just as entitled to success. She would have been able to assert herself without letting perceived flaws and shortcomings hold her back.

Everyone is different, but if you consider yourself lower down in the hierarchy, it will be impossible to stand up for your rights and ask for the treatment and respect you deserve. You can't turn people down and put yourself first if your insecurities grant them undeserved power over you.

Your Personal Bill of Rights

They may start with the same four letters, but self-prioritization, self-compassion, and self-acceptance are not the same as being selfish. These aren't privileges that it's selfish to chase. They're your rights, things you utterly deserve to have.

It's your responsibility to assert your personal bill of rights, as no one is going to do it for you. You can't depend on people to consider how they might be infringing on them, as they'll be focusing on how they can achieve their own satisfaction. Being able to say, "I know my rights," allows you to assert yourself in order to fulfill them.

The accumulation of contorted messages saying you must be selfless to be a good person leads to feeling guilty or selfish for asserting these rights. Losing sight of your personal bill of rights happens because of the conditioning that forces you to believe you should put others before yourself.

As you read the rights described below, notice whether any of them surprise you. You'll realize that actions or phrases you have been afraid of using for fear of seeming flakey, selfish, rude, or stupid are actually your *rights*. They are the key to being assertive because they give you permission to act as your authentic self, guilt-free.

It's your right to not justify your behavior with excuses.

You don't have to give reasons or agree to things you don't want to do because you're worried that your reason doesn't seem good enough. If you don't want to attend an event because you want to spend quality time with your dog, that's valid and no one can judge. You don't owe someone something just because your justification doesn't align with their values.

It's your right to change your mind.

What was possible when you agreed to something might not be possible anymore. This is normal in a world where things are constantly changing. It's a shame to inconvenience someone, but you have to look after yourself.

It's your right to say, "I don't know."

Capable people often have the burden of problem-solver thrust upon them by people who have the ability to find the solution but don't want to put the time in. You don't have to go out of your way to find answers to things that aren't useful to you. You might be expected to know, but even the experts come across a topic they're unsure of from time to time.

It's your right to be illogical in your decision-making.

If you've saved for years for a house and one day decide to blow it all on a trip round the world, that's up to you. Others' expectations of you based on patterns of your previous behavior aren't something you have to conform to forever. It simply doesn't matter if no one can understand why you're doing something.

It's your right to decide which of other people's problems you have a responsibility to solve.

No matter how persuasive the cries of "You have to help me!" may be, only you can make that choice. If you have the time and resources to help someone, then this can be a positive experience for you both, but you need defenses in place to prevent you from feeling pressured, blackmailed, or helpless.

It's your right to say, "I don't understand."

Not everyone will give clear instructions or remember what it was like to tackle a new subject for the first time. There's no obligation on you to understand everything. In a work setting, you may worry that saying you don't understand will make you look incompetent, but they hired you for a reason. Self-acceptance involves knowing what you know, and being honest will help you to learn and grow rather than pretending you understand something you don't.

It's your right to say, "I don't care."

There will always be people who drain you and demand your attention for every little drama in their life. There are only so many good causes you can champion. You have to draw the line somewhere: for everything you don't care about, there will be someone else who does care and can do what you're not willing to.

You've now seen just how many things you deserve that you've been missing out on because you haven't realized that the only person who can provide them all is yourself. You deserve to prioritize yourself and be the hero in your own movie—not the martyr who gives their life to save everyone else. Prioritizing time for you to meet your own needs and giving up the pursuit of altruism will improve your well-being. You can't please everyone all the time, so start with yourself, which is the first step to assertiveness.

Takeaways:

1. Nobody else in your life will ever put you first, at least not in the way you deserve to be. This starts with self-prioritization. Altruism is an admirable trait, but only in balance can you be assertive for yourself.

2. Self-compassion is where you put your own feelings and thoughts before those of others—for example, your happiness over the annoyance or disappointment of others.

3. Self-acceptance is the knowledge that you are good enough, deserving, and worthy of your own needs. How can you ever assert yourself if you don't feel like you're good enough? You might just feel like you deserve nothing.

4. Write the personal bill of rights down and post it on a wall in your room. These are rights, not privileges or luxuries. It's easy to forget until someone snaps you out of it.

Chapter 4. How to Ask for What You Want and Get It

Meghan's birthday was last Friday. Her husband, Tim, asked her what she wanted to do, but she was noncommittal and said anything would be fine. Secretly, however, Meghan started imagining what the evening might entail: a drive downtown, a walk through a few quaint little shops, a quiet dinner with wine and a special delivery of flowers right to the table, intriguing conversation, and tender kisses under the stars—a perfect night.

Tim, who was determined to make the night special, tried to remember some of the things he had heard Meghan mention over the last few weeks. After careful planning, he was sure she would love his idea. So why was Meghan so upset when Tim announced they were taking the kids to the circus, then trying out the new bowling alley and pizza parlor down near the university to celebrate?

Meghan wanted a quiet, romantic, kid-free birthday celebration; Tim wanted to show her he had paid attention when she mentioned the circus was in town and that she had heard the new bowling alley had her favorite— Chicago-style pizza. Meghan was trying not to seem demanding; Tim was trying to guess what she wanted. Unfortunately, he was wrong, and both parties ended up unhappy and annoyed.

Could this situation have been improved with assertiveness? It seems so simple and even easy, but this is probably not an unfamiliar situation. One of the biggest reasons people fail to get what they want is by failing to ask for what they want. For all the reasons we've covered in this book thus far, we just don't want to put ourselves in that position.

Speak Up

Clearly, the most effective way of increasing assertiveness is to get better at asking for what you want. You didn't need to read this far in the book for this type of amazing insight.

When people fail to speak up and ask for what they want, they are not saying, "I don't care" or "It doesn't matter to me." What they are saying, and more significantly, what they are believing is, "I don't feel comfortable" or "I don't feel worthy." Whatever the case, they feel that more negativity will arise than positivity if they make a perfectly reasonable request. In order to become more assertive, both of those thoughts need to vanish.

In the example above, Meghan could have been hearing either one of those phrases in her mind. Maybe she did not feel comfortable asking for a quiet dinner out because she knew it would mean spending money on a sitter, driving away from their neighborhood, or doing things she was not sure Tim would enjoy. Maybe she did not feel worthy because a date like she imagined would include her being the center of Tim's attention, and she was not sure he would want to spend an evening like that. Either way, because she did not make her preference known, she was disappointed, and Tim went to a lot of effort only to disappoint her. Happy birthday to no one.

Before speaking up and asking for what you want, you need to recognize that you feel uncomfortable or unworthy. Often, these are subconscious thoughts—habits, even—that form from a lifetime of not asking for what you want. Other times, this might be a look into your psyche and how you actually view yourself as compared to others.

Becoming comfortable asking for what you want, especially if you are not used to doing so, takes practice. There are no magic phrases; it is a matter of identifying what your desired outcome is and then finding the words to ask for it. Had Meghan just said something like, "I'd like a quiet dinner with just us," Tim, unless he is completely clueless, would not have planned going to the circus followed by pizza and bowling.

They Should Have Known

Perhaps in an alternative universe, people are so intuitive they can accurately predict the desires of others, but in this time and day, there are not many psychics. We are all guilty of making assumptions and dropping subtle hints. Yet these methods do not usually lead to us getting our desires because there's no reason to expect people to be able to read your minds and desires, even if you've been married for 20 years.

Harville Hendricks, a prominent couples therapist, theorizes that people believe this myth of being able to read another person's desires comes from the way parents try to determine the needs of babies. The reality is, when a baby cries, most parents have no idea why. What they do know, however, is that there are a limited number of things that could be wrong. If they try feeding, changing a diaper, or shifting positions, chances are the baby will stop crying. It's not that parents have magical intuitive powers; it's that after a few weeks, they learn what causes the baby to cry and what helps him stop crying. They have been conditioned to respond in specific ways to their baby's cries.

As children grow and become more verbal, parents can still sense when something is wrong, but that does not mean they can read their child's mind. Most mature people recognize and admit that they cannot read the minds of others, yet somehow mature, intelligent adults struggle with communicating their own needs because they believe the other person should intuitively know what to do or say.

Thus, our expectations become skewed. Most of the time, people do not give voice to their expectations because there is a belief that they should not have to say it out loud.

Think about how ridiculous this seems. *If he really knows me, then he should know that I want a romantic date, not a trip to the circus, for my birthday celebration.* And yet, this becomes a source of conflict in many relationships. One person has an expectation and believes the other person should have a similar expectation—even though they never discuss it. In the end, someone is disappointed; in fact, both are probably disappointed.

People are hurt over and over because they have hopes concerning a certain situation, but the result is different from that expectation. Consider Frances and Dave. They have been friends since college, but when Frances loses his father to cancer, their friendship nearly ends. Dave knows his friend has responsibilities taking care of his father's business, so he tries to stay out of the way. Frances, on the other hand, really wants to spend time with people who knew his dad and will help preserve his memory. Dave thinks he is helping; Frances thinks Dave is being a lousy friend.

These instances happen regularly and there is only one reason they happen: people don't assert their expectations. Being furious for someone because *they should have known* does not count.

Expecting people to know expectations and desires without telling them is a bit like emotional hostage-taking. When people do not speak up and share what they want, they are essentially highjacking the relationship. After all, the chances of the other person getting it just right without being told are pretty slim.

Misunderstandings can fester and grow to the point they metastasize into a cancer of disappointment that can poison an entire relationship. No matter the situation, when expectations are not met, individuals eventually reach a point where they can no longer be silent. Often it boils over into a huge fight with accusations from the past flying wildly. The worst of these arguments can include ugly words and hateful statements that can never be taken back.

Everyone has different expectations, narratives, stories, and perspectives. Thus, things that are quite insignificant like gas or laundry or family time or birthday celebrations become symbolic of the much deeper yet real issue. When we give "symbolic value" to action, or lack of action, we not only risk our own disappointment, but we also set up our partner to fail.

Symbolic Value

Often people fail to recognize the symbolic value they place on certain actions. Except for being polite, there is no *real* value on opening the door for someone. The value is in the *symbol* of opening the door. It can symbolize respect, care, a desire to make an impression—a whole host of things. *It's about the principle of the matter!* Symbolic value is most significant to the person on the receiving end of the act, and it's a primary reason why you become offended when people don't read your mind.

Nick and Michelle have an agreement that he will be responsible for getting the garbage out for collection each week. When Nick fails to do his job, Michelle feels like he is purposely telling her that he does not intend to keep his end of the bargain. She thinks he is being disrespectful to her by sending the message "Whatever I was doing was more important than keeping my promise to you." In all likelihood, Nick is just forgetful, but that's not what Michelle feels. She starts imagining what other promises he will fail to keep. Before long, she is hurt and angry.

Because Michelle places such a high symbolic value on it, she assumes Nick knows how important it is to her. What's more, she thinks Nick has the same symbolic values as her, which should naturally inform his decisions. When they argue about it, Nick will think they are arguing about the trash, but Michelle will think they are arguing about how he has stomped on her feelings. The combination of putting symbolic value on the trash and making assumptions that the other person understands that value has the potential to turn this into an ongoing battle.

Are you allowing yourself to be upset by assigning symbolic value to things and waiting for people to perform them before you ever have to assert yourself? You are just making yourself vulnerable to hurt, especially if you're unaware of what you assign symbolic value to. This is what you're allowing to happen when you don't assert yourself.

Can you simply change someone's behavior like Pavlov's dog and bypass having to assert yourself and make your desires known? Sometimes instead of open and honest communication, people will try to change the other person's behavior. Unfortunately, that does not usually work.

In Nick and Michelle's case, Michelle could reward Nick for taking care of the garbage. She could prepare his favorite snack and drink after he returns from the curb; she could vocalize her appreciation by thanking him or praising him to others; she could do something that has symbolic value for him in return. If this sounds a bit like training a puppy or teaching a child how to behave, it's because it is; it's classical conditioning, and she is attempting to condition Nick into having the same symbolic values as her.

Do what I want and get a reward. It's not exactly a mature way to deal with problems in a relationship and won't work as neatly as with rats, a maze, and cheese.

There is only one way to turn your expectations into reality. You have to speak your mind and ask for what you want. The key to success, however, is doing that without being passive-aggressive.

Passive-Aggression

Passive-aggressive behavior is a common technique people use to get their way instead of actual assertiveness. It happens when people sugarcoat their hostility. Instead of being honest with people, a passive-aggressive person will send a message that says the opposite of how they feel. They hide their anger (and aggression) beneath a compliant exterior that is designed to create action. *Oh, not a problem that you're late, I just had to reschedule my appointment, which was super hard to obtain to next year!*

Instead of dealing with an issue straight on, people who need to have a confrontation but are afraid of it attempt to make a point under a cloak of niceness. It is the opposite of assertiveness and more similar to preferring that people read your mind. Passive-aggressive behavior can be referred to as hostile cooperation, but in reality, it is not cooperation at all. It is an expression of anger masked as something else (Long, Long & Whitson, 2008).

When people deal with others passive-aggressively, they rarely end up getting what they want. Avoiding passive-aggressive behavior means dealing with honest feelings instead of letting them leak out bit by bit. When you're angry, be angry and deal with it. Get rid of jabs and barbs while being clear, honest, and communicative; make your intentions and your message clear. Do not assume your partner is choosing to ignore your needs and make you angry; instead deal with the anger and set the stage for progress. Taking a passive-aggressive stance and hoping your partner catches the hint is a recipe for disaster.

Back to Nick and Michelle and their garbage. Both Nick and Michelle could behave in a passive-aggressive way. Nick, could deliberately "forget" to take out the trash because he feels like Michelle nags and disrespects him. The trash is a way to get back at her by giving her a dose of her own medicine. Michelle could choose to give Nick the silent treatment and refuse to discuss her feelings when Nick tries to get her to talk about what is wrong.

Or consider Sean and Tamara. Sean enjoys going to a coffee shop to catch up on some blogs he follows. Tamara says he disappears every time she needs him to help get their twins ready for dance class. Sean has placed symbolic value on his time alone, and Tamara has placed symbolic value on Sean helping with their kids. Sean agrees to skip his time at the coffee shop, but instead of helping prepare for dance class, he busies himself with other distractions.

Tamara starts making snide remarks every time she asks Sean for help. Words like "Sean, can you do the dishes—if you're not going to

Starbucks?" or "After that fourth cup of coffee, would you mind reading a blog with the kids?" In their passive-aggression, both remain angry, frustrated, and unsatisfied.

Becoming Assertive the Right Way

All of the people mentioned in this chapter are examples of real people with real hurt feelings. Trying to modify another adult's behavior is probably not going to work. Hoping they can suddenly peer into your mind is also likely a recipe for failure. Being passive-aggressive is going to make the problems these people face worse instead of better. Learning to ask for you want is key.

There is an easy fix to these disruptions in relationships. It *is* as simple as opening your mouth and saying out loud what you want. Simple statements like "I would like you to wash the dishes while I help the kids with their homework" or "I would like to spend some time alone with you; let's get a sitter and plan a night out" actually work the vast majority of the time.

(1) Don't fill the silence after your assertive request that you perceive to be gaping and awkward—that's where it's too easy for us to hedge and say things like, "Only if you want!" or "But I could go either way; it's up to you, really." It's in this moment of weakness that most of us fail, even when we have a strong start.

(2) In a *Psychology Today* piece, psychologist Susan Krauss Whitbourn suggests that, when asking for something, it is crucial to consider the person we are asking.

- Are their needs being considered?
- How can this request benefit them?
- Is this a good time to make such a request?
- If the tables were turned, how would I view this request?

By considering these questions, it becomes easier to frame the request in a way that could make it seem more appealing and overall like less of an ask. Hey, if you're going to assert yourself, you can at least make it seem like you're barely making a request.

For example, someone in the middle of a stressful personal ordeal might not feel that she can take on another project at work. Hinting around that she should take on an intern is likely to be ignored. However, a direct conversation about how an intern could be utilized to reduce some of her daily tasks and allow her to focus on something more important to her might allow her to see an opportunity to focus on work she loves while allowing someone else to manage some of her day-to-day grunt work.

Assertiveness can be made much more palatable if you just take into account what the other person wants to feel and think. Are you really making a request if the other person stands to benefit as well? It sure feels better.

(3) Likewise, assertiveness can flow when you make your requests convenient and easy. If you need to meet face to face, do it at their office, on their break, or at their favorite lunch spot. Do not expect them to go out of their way in order for you to request a favor. Instead of your natural inclination to hedge with "Can we meet? Only if you have time," you can substitute it with "Can we meet? Lunch is on me at your favorite sandwich place."

(4) Offer clear-cut options.

If you are asking someone to help with a charity fundraiser, have options they can choose from; if you are asking for someone to watch your dog, offer to take him to their place or let them stay at your place and use your building's gym facilities while you are out of town. Also, make sure they have a way to say no without feeling guilty in case they cannot or do not want to do what you have asked. It may be a great charity, but they might have other causes they support; they might love your dog but do not want the responsibility of caring for a pet.

Make sure they can see the work you have put in before making the request. Show the research you have done on the charity or make sure they know who is willing to take the dog in case of an emergency. Don't just ask for something and expect someone to do all the dirty work and research for you.

(5) Whitbourn also notes the importance of asking for one thing when the real intention is something else. Having an ulterior motive is hard to hide. Being direct and honest about what you want and why you want it allows for effective communication.

It might be difficult to imagine why a person would express a desire without being honest about it, but it does happen. Anyone who owns a pickup truck knows what it's like to be called upon to first catch up and then magically to help a friend move a couple of things. It starts with a sofa and then, next thing you know, it's also a dozen boxes, a refrigerator, and a bike.

This is going to feel like a covert operation. It's dishonest and is going to make the owner of the truck feel used or set up. It's because there was a guise of friendship and wanting to catch up, which was quickly discarded as a front. Contrast this to be being direct and straightforward about your request. There is greater chance of being refused—this is what we innately want to prevent and avoid—but when it is accepted, it is accepted on its merits and without bitterness or resentment. A dishonest request will lead to far worse feelings in the long run than an honest request.

(6) Finally, be specific.

When people give general requests, imagine how that sounds to the recipient of the request. It's basically open-ended, and they aren't completely sure of what they will be agreeing and obligating themselves to. "Can you help out with the bake sale" is a vague, scary request that you should rightfully not assert. "Can you bring cupcakes to the bake sale and man the table for one hour?" is something that is specific, easier to say yes to, and will get a more positive and thoughtful reaction as opposed to a blanket no. In making requests, you have to combine common sense and strategy.

(7) Oh, and if someone says no? You better not pout.

If you pout and get upset when someone turns down what you perceive to be a reasonable request, you go on people's black lists. A small percentage of people might cave in once they see you've become upset, but pouting is actually a subtle form of emotional blackmail like we talked about earlier—the self-punisher's threat "If I don't get what I want from you, I will make myself suffer."

For the rest of us, no one wants to be around someone who sulks around when things do not go as planned. People who act entitled do not win friends. In fact, people who feel and act resentful seem petty, immature, and whiny rather than mature and responsible.

Being assertive does mean always getting your way. But when you take time to articulate reasonable requests, chances are good that they will be met. Sometimes the timing is off or other factors need to be considered, but that is not a reason to ruminate over a disappointing outcome. When things do not work out, it is easy to feel sorry for yourself; that can lower your self-esteem and lead to feelings of depression. In fact, some people would even start to question whether or not they should have asserted themselves in the first place.

In the end, one of the best ways to improve assertiveness is to consider what you want in a particular situation, decide the best time and place to make your request known, speak up for yourself, and then negotiate for a solution that meets the needs of all of those involved. In that way, you make assertiveness seem harmless and burdenless.

Takeaways:

1. How do you ask for what you want? Well, you already know how. But we don't for various reasons, the first of which is that they should have known. They should have been able to read our minds and understand and anticipate our needs. Yes, in fairy tales, but not in reality.

2. We also wait for people to take action because of the symbolic value we assign to things. We believe other people's symbolic value matches ours, which should inform their actions. But this is again projecting

onto other people and depending on them to read our minds. We also can't subtly try to condition people into feeling the same symbolic value as us.

3. Passive-aggressive behavior is concealed hostility masquerading as niceness, often with the goal of inducing some type of behavior. This happens when people are too angry to ask for what they want, typically.

4. There are better and worse ways to making requests and asking for what you want. In fact, there are seven elements that will help you the most. Don't fill the silence after your ask, consider the other person's needs, make it easy and convenient, offer clear options, be direct and honest, be specific, and don't you dare pout if you get turned down.

Chapter 5. Saying N-O Without Tension

Jack was terrified when he saw his friend Carlo walking toward him on the street. Jack and Carlo were friends since childhood. Yet when Jack saw Carlo approaching him with a smile on his face, Jack wished he had the grit to turn and run away as fast as he could. He knew what was coming.

Jack had heard a rumor from mutual friends that Carlo would soon be moving to yet another apartment. This would be Carlo's fourth apartment in the last four years. With each of Carlo's moves, Jack had been recruited to be part of Carlo's moving crew.

Jack had grown weary of the task. Helping Carlo move was a lot of work. Jack compared it to a labor camp. There was no pay, and the only reward Jack got for his efforts was pizza and beer.

Carlo had plenty of money to pay a moving company for such a task, but it seems that he was either too frugal to do so or he thought his select group of friends enjoyed helping him with the lengthy and laborious task of moving.

Jack didn't mind helping people. He had a good heart. But he was at a point now where he thought that Carlo was taking advantage of his inability to say no. Last time he had helped Carlo move, Jack had strained his back—not enough to quit working, but enough so that he was both stiff and sore when he and Carlo's other friends finished the move. Carlo laughed it off and told him to buy some Advil. And Jack was so busy with his life now that he wasn't sure he had a full day to spare to help Carlo with another move. Jack was now helping to care for his elderly father and his free time had become more precious than ever.

"Jack, my old buddy, how are you doing?" smiled Carlo as he finally reached his friend. "You're just the man I want to see. I have a favor to ask of you."

Jack knew the question before it was asked. He also knew that Carlo was a persistent sort, someone who would not easily take no for an answer. "What's that, Carlo?" Jack replied.

"I'm moving to a new apartment complex at the end of the month and I could really use your help with that. Can I count on your help?"

Jack surprised himself by replying without hesitation. "Not this time, Carlo. I've been helping my sister care for my father. He broke his hip a couple weeks ago and he needs someone to tend to him around the clock. I just don't have the time to spare. I'll have to take a raincheck. Maybe next time. So how have you been, Carlo?" Jack was proud of himself for his resolve in saying no. And he was also proud to know that he had quickly changed the subject after he declined the invitation, leaving no room for further discussion.

You may have that same fear that Jack had—the fear of saying no.

Learning to say no can be the ultimate assertive skill a person can possess. Most of us aim to please. We've often found that it can be easier to say yes than to say no. When we say no, we realize that we bring negativity and possible confrontation or disappointment into an interaction.

There are some main reasons that people don't like to say no:

- We're afraid of being rude.
- We want to be agreeable. We don't want to alienate ourselves from the individual or the group making the request.
- We're afraid of conflict. Maybe the person or persons making the request will get angry if we reject their request. This might lead to an ugly or unpleasant confrontation. Many of us try to avoid confrontations as much as possible.

- We don't want to burn bridges. Some people take no as a sign of personal rejection and they may decide to hold your lack of cooperation against you.
- We like to be helpful. It feels good. But at what price? Our time is valuable.

"I Can't" vs. "I Don't"

You might be surprised to know that how we talk to ourselves can impact our ability to say no. *The Journal of Consumer Research* published a study in which 120 students were divided into two groups—the "I can't" group and the "I don't" group. One group was told that each time they were faced with temptation they were to tell themselves, "I can't do X." For example, when tempted with chocolate, they were to say, "I can't eat chocolate." The other group, the "I don't" group, was instructed to say, "I don't do X" or, in the case of chocolate, "I don't eat chocolate."

The results of this study showed the major impact that just a slight difference in vocabulary can make on our ability to say no, to resist temptation, and to motivate goal-directed behavior. The "I don't" group was overwhelming more successful in its ability to say no.

If you tell yourself "I can't," you're simply reminding yourself of the limitations you've set for yourself. You're creating a feedback loop in your brain that tells you that you can't do something that you would normally want to do. "I can't" becomes an exercise in self-discipline, which is not something you want to constantly depend on.

On the other hand, when you tell yourself "I don't," you're creating a feedback loop that reminds you of your power and control of the situation. You've given yourself a line in the sand that takes the situation out of your hands. Your choice was premade to say no and thus you can stick to it more easily. By simply changing one word when we talk to ourselves, we can change our behavior. When people hear "don't," it's more of a hard boundary, whereas "can't" typically implies an open-ended answer that encourages people to try to persuade and coax you.

For example, consider a situation in which someone on a diet is offered a calorie-loaded dessert. If they say "I can't," they are reminding themselves of the limitations created by their diet. They have thought about it and made an active decision to say no. If they instead say "I don't" when offered the same dessert, they'll be taking control of the situation and only have to stick to their premade decision. They'll be reminding themselves that they don't eat foods that are full of calories.

The "I don't" mantra can be an invaluable tool in our daily lives. In saying "I don't let my friends talk me into things I don't want to do" or "I don't eat between meals," we make it a lot easier to say no or resist temptation. We also empower ourselves and make it much easier to achieve our goals and objectives. We are talking both to ourselves and the requesters.

You've got a policy and you're sticking it!

Rejecting Categories

In learning to say no, the same "I don't" principle applies to someone who gets repeated requests for favors or obligations. Instead of reviewing each request separately, you might consider rejecting the entire category.

In other words, instead of reviewing each request and making an "I can" or an "I can't" decision, you'll find that it's much more empowering to reject all requests that are in a certain category, such as "Sorry, I don't do those types of meetings anymore."

This approach will take all of the decision-making out of requests from other people and you'll find that it's much easier to say no to these requests. Yes, you can make exceptions to requests when it's something you really want to do or really need to do, but you'll find that it will be much easier to opt in to a request than it is to opt out. Just like with saying "I don't" as opposed to "I can't," refusing an entire category is a boundary that most people will accept. If they sense you make exceptions frequently, they will attempt to persuade you to let them be yet another one.

As an example, our old friend Jack is a well-known author whose crime novels have sold hundreds of thousands of copies. As a result, he gets numerous requests from groups who invite him to attend their meetings and discuss these books. Inundated with requests from groups as small as five or six people and as large as 200 people, Jack has established his own criteria for speaking to groups about his books. He won't speak to any groups of less than 20 and he won't make any group presentations in the months of May through August, as those are the months he wants to use to write his next book and those are also months when his kids are out of school and he wants to make sure he spends time with them then.

In forming his own restrictive criteria to filter guest speaking requests, Jack finds it much easier to say no to many of the numerous requests he receives. He already knows what his rules are, and it's easier to abide to a blanket rule than decide who deserves to be an exception.

Once again, if it's difficult for you to say no, you should resolve to start rejecting categories. Resolve to say no whenever someone asks you for a favor. Automatically reject the request, categorically. Then, if it is something you really want to do, you can always opt in and say yes. But no should be your preferred response.

If you have people in your life that make repeated requests, it might be better to preempt their request. "I know you're moving at the end of the month. If you need help moving, I'll have to take a raincheck this time around. My wife and I agreed that we should make an effort to spend more time with the kids."

Examine Your Beliefs

Another thing to consider as you learn to say no is to examine your beliefs. What do you believe will happen when you say no?

Will you be burned at the stake? Chances are low.

Hanged in effigy? Executed? Probably not.

Even Carlo, who doesn't like to take no for an answer, will eventually move on and honor your decision. If you say no to someone, they're likely to accept your decision, at least eventually. Oh, they may be angry with you for a while. They may even hate you for a while. But eventually they'll get over it and go along with your decision. The point is that you should take care that your beliefs are reasonable and balanced and realize that saying no will never end the world or cause everything you fear to come into being. Saying no is reasonable and even normal, and isn't a last resort for when you have no other choice.

Obviously, there are limits here. If you're part of a family, is it always reasonable for you to say no to help with the cleaning? Probably not. If you're part of an athletic team, is it fair for you to only think of your personal goals? Certainly not. You should examine your beliefs and make sure they are reasonable enough and balanced enough to coincide with those around you.

Overall, gain awareness around the consequences of saying no and what you believe will happen. For example, if you have some friends who keep asking you to join them for a night out on the town, and you keep telling them that you can't go, for whatever reason, you should know that they'll eventually stop inviting you. That may be okay with you if you don't enjoy those gatherings or the company, but if you do enjoy them, you should know the eventual consequences of continuing to decline those invitations.

So whenever you say no to someone or something, you should be aware of how your decision will affect those around you and also the consequences that decision will have on you and others. But as we'll discuss next, don't forget that it's okay to be selfish sometimes.

Maintain Your Personal Space

Being able to say no isn't just a nice skill to have; it's also a good way to create and keep your personal space. In fact, that's often the point we are trying to make. In doing this, we have to remember that it's okay to be selfish sometimes; it's okay to prioritize yourself.

Here's an example. As a recent college graduate now working in a major company, Phillip found that he was often being stretched between his old college friends and his coworkers. Just about every weekend, Phillip would receive social invitations from both his college friends and his work friends. He often felt like he was in the middle of a tug-of-war, with friends on both sides tugging at him, his time, and his space.

He enjoyed both his college friends and his work friends, but there were many times when he just wanted to spend some weekend time to himself, doing things he wanted to do. Eventually he grew weary, burnt out from all the socializing. So he decided to take back his personal space and his free time.

He set boundaries for himself and he was open about letting his friends know he wasn't interested in going out every weekend. After he set those boundaries, Phillip was happy to have some occasional time to himself. He still went out with his buddies, but he did so on his terms. He didn't go out because he felt compelled to do so. He did so because he wanted to do so. And when he went because he wanted to go, Phillip enjoyed his social time even more, as he didn't feel guilty about taking away from his own time.

Phillip later admitted to himself that it wasn't his friends' fault. They didn't know what his agenda was. How were they to know? And they all had their own agendas. He, too, had his own agenda and he, too, needed to maintain his own personal space.

In saying no, it's okay to make it about you sometimes. After all, it's your time, your sanity, your wallet, your availability, your choice.

Keep It Simple

The best way to say no is to be simple and straightforward. There are no tricks around how to do it; it's just the inherent discomfort and tension of the act.

If you've been passive for a long time, people are going to be surprised when you say no. And if you're dealing with someone who has an alpha personality, they will almost surely try to get you to change your decision. Heck, your lack of assertiveness might by why they hang around you in the first place, and it's tough to change that relationship dynamic once it's been set. Expect pushback and shock when you change the dynamic.

The worst thing you can do in such a predicament is revise your decision. If you do, you'll know that you'll have to face the same predicament with the same person whenever they have future requests. And they'll know that your no is negotiable. Become a broken record. Each time they ask, answer with a quick and simple no, leaving no room for negotiation. If you appear to have wiggle room, you'll just be encouraging people to continue to persuade you.

Resist the moment

The toughest time in saying no usually occurs right after you do so. It's then when you want to offer help, keep talking, or do anything to reduce the tension that your no has created. This is usually the time when you start wavering: "Well, if you really need my help, I guess I could . . ." "I'd rather not, but . . ." Resist the temptation and stay silent, because your assertiveness is often lost in that moment.

When saying no, remember that you don't need to make excuses. You can say you're busy, it's not in your wheelhouse, or whatever your reason is, but that's it. Leave it at that. If you still feel the need to add a "because" at the end of your sentence, keep it short and simple and don't elaborate on the details. The more details you give, the more fodder you give people to pick at. For instance, if you say no to helping a friend move because you need to walk your cat in the morning, you create an avenue for people to dispute that you need to walk a cat at all.

Don't hem and haw your way through a lame explanation on why you said no. Don't feel compelled to share an alternative or something that can make up for your no. It's okay to just say no. No further explanation is needed. Overall, remember that no can be a complete sentence.

Create hoops

If you can't just say no or if you can't say no immediately, another option is to defer the decision or punt it into the future. Tell them you'll think about it, and if applicable, ask them to do something to prepare you for it. In other words, put the burden back on them by requesting something to help you consider their request. Confused?

Let's take Jonathan, who is very smart and mentors companies. He is asked for coffee all the time from people who would like to "pick his brain" and otherwise soak up information from him like a sponge. As you can imagine, he doesn't have time for everyone that asks him. He has to say no quite frequently, but he's devised a way around it. He creates a hoop for them to jump through before agreeing to anything further. When someone asks him for coffee, he will ask them to send, via email, an agenda or plan of what they want to discuss and why. He doesn't hear from 99% of the people again.

As you can see in Jonathan's case, it becomes very clear who just wants to use you for something without being willing to contribute in any way or make it easy for you. When someone asks you for something, create a condition for them to fulfill in order for you to consider their request. It will buy you time and space, and most people will never get back to you because they would have to put in the work!

Bait and switch

Another option, if you're having a tough time saying no, will be to offer a bait and switch yes: "I can't do that, but I can do this."

"I can't spend all day helping you move to another apartment, but I can give you two hours."

"I can't go out with you this weekend, but I promise that I'll make some time to do that within the next month."

"I can't serve on the board, but I'll be willing to consult on an ad-hoc basis whenever I have time."

What you're doing here is saying no to the request and offering a smaller consolation prize that may or may not be refused. It may be a legitimate alternative as something you are willing to do, but it doesn't have to be.

Your no is disguised because you appear to be still open and willing, at least on the surface. If you offer something relatively small, people will likely refuse and tell you not to bother with it. Even better is if you don't provide specific detail and leave it as open-ended as possible. In most cases, the bait and switch will result in freedom from an ask or obligation. This tactic alleviates most of the tension because you are saying yes to something, just not what is specifically being asked.

Keep it nonpersonal

Many times when we say no, it feels terrible because we know how we'd feel when we get rejected. We might take it personally and ruminate on how much someone doesn't care about us or perhaps how the symbolic value is lacking. Therefore, it's important to keep your no as nonpersonal as possible and as focused on the specific situation at hand as possible.

In essence, you are rejecting the person because of the situation and circumstances, not because of the person themselves. Some people have difficulty separating the two, but the former is much, much easier to both speak and hear.

For instance, you are invited to a friend's party, only to learn that your ex, with whom you had a particularly nasty split, will be there. Your friend is giving you grief about passing it up, but in reality, it's not about your friend: it's about the situation and being in an enclosed area with someone who makes you nauseous. In this case, you would emphasize that you aren't saying no to spending time with your friend, which is what they might perceive, but instead saying no to being in your ex's presence.

A little bit of regret always helps—for instance, "I'd really love to and I was really looking forward to hanging out with you, but I can't!" When people feel validated and not rejected, they'll accept a no far more easily. Just be sure to focus on the specific circumstance and how they won't work for you.

Pass the buck

Here, you aren't saying no as much as "Yes, but . . ." Allow me to explain. Passing the buck means passing the responsibility onto someone else who is not you.

It's when you suggest that someone else would be a much better, more qualified fit than you, and thus, you should bow out. You wouldn't do the requester justice, but you can still help them solve their problem by finding someone who will. The requester won't necessary hear a no, which is the most important part.

For instance, if you are asking someone to drive you to the airport, you might say, "No, I'm a terrible driver and driving on the

111

highways make me feel anxious, but Ted is a great driver and might be free that day!" You've successfully passed the buck to Ted by making yourself pale in comparison to how Ted might solve the issue.

People ask you for things because they want to solve a problem they have. If you make yourself seem like a terrible solution, but at the same time can point them in the direction of a real solution, you've avoided a duty.

Saying no is a valuable skill. In learning to say no, you'll be able to take control of your life and your time. In learning to say no, you'll empower yourself to avoid the things you don't want to do. In learning to say no properly, you'll be able to avoid tension, confrontation, and ruffled feathers. A life devoid of no is one that is not your own; it is one that is lived for other people.

Like any skill, the ability to say no is often an acquired talent. When Jack told Carlo he would not be able to help him move at the end of the month, he was able to do so because he was resolute in his statement.

Jack didn't leave Carlo with the idea that this decision was open for discussion.

You, too, can learn how to say no. It may take some time and some practice, but when you become proficient at saying no, you'll wonder what to do with all the free time you now possess.

Takeaways:

1. Saying no is one of the toughest situations in everyday life because it is a mini confrontation every single time. But there are many ways to make this part of life smoother and less tense.

2. Start saying "I don't" versus "I can't" because the former implies a policy, whereas the latter implies something to be negotiated. Likewise, get into the habit of saying no to specific and broad categories because that also implies a policy that you don't make exceptions for.

3. It's important to also examine your beliefs surrounding no and what happens when you agree or disagree. Importantly, you must think about how you maintain your

personal space and balance the demands of other people. The cost-benefit analysis will come up very strongly in your favor.

4. There are countless ways to say no. You already know a few, including the simplest way: "no" as a complete sentence. Understand that people will react strongly to you if you have a history of people-pleasing and being a doormat.

5. Other methods of saying no include resisting the moment where you want to insert an addendum or caveat, creating hoops for people to jump through and themselves say yes to, baiting and switching with related or unrelated tasks, keeping it nonpersonal and focused on the specific circumstance, and passing the buck to someone who appears to be able to solve the problem at hand much better than you.

Chapter 6. The Need to Please

If you were to read a review of yourself, perhaps in an appraisal at work, you might be pleased to see yourself described as "accommodating" and "agreeable." This might be a good review at work, but are they generally good words to be described with? Be careful, as you might be fooled with the misplaced positivity around them.

To be accommodating or agreeable means adapting to make others happy, which isn't establishing boundaries—it's people-pleasing.

Accommodating people can be seen as less trustworthy because they change depending on who they're talking to. It's hard to trust someone with an important task if you know that they'll instantly make the next person who asks for help their top priority. They're perceived as being weak, easily manipulated, and unable to take the reins and pull rank when a problem occurs.

If an employee suspects their accommodating employee's motive is just to make people happy and tell them what they want to hear, it's unlikely they will be tasked with handling difficult, high-stakes negotiations with important clients.

It's not bad to be agreeable, and often this comes from a place of empathy—a psychological desire to create social harmony and trying to make life better for everyone else.

Agreeableness can also come from a desire to be liked, resulting in a lack of genuineness and suppression of the self. In an interesting display of the complexity of human nature, most people are actually annoyed by people-pleasing.

In a 2010 study published in the *Journal of Personality and Social Psychology*, researchers analyzed people's reactions to selfish versus generous actions in a game about rewards. They found that instead of appreciating the generous players, these were actually as equally disliked as the selfish ones.

The unselfish members who gave toward the provision of a public good but used little of it themselves were also excluded from the group. Two follow-up studies were conducted, which found it wasn't unpredictability or confusion causing these results. People just found the generous players as unlikeable as the selfish ones.

It seemed that these agreeable players made other people feel bad about themselves. They were also deemed "rule-breakers." Although they were breaking the rules of negative social norms in a positive way, it was too much. Trying to be too nice, whether to impress or due to a craving for social harmony, actually caused people to exclude them from the very group they wanted to help.

You may have tried taking on the dirty jobs nobody else wants or paying a bar tab at a work party in the hope it would endear you to a group. This is actually likely to have the opposite effect; your extreme generosity makes people just as uncomfortable as the selfish people who make life more difficult or refuse to contribute.

Going against the grain, even if that's by doing good deeds, makes you stand out as a target. You're actually just as likely as the selfish person to be recommended for voluntary redundancy or to find there never seems to be room for you in any of the cars on road trips.

University of Notre Dame Researchers in 2011 found that disagreeable employees earned more than their agreeable counterparts. Disagreeable men earned 18% more than agreeable men. Agreeableness is a more socially expected norm in women, but disagreeable women still earned 5% more than the agreeable women, and these agreeable women lagged far behind the disagreeable men.

Agreeable people do just that: they agree, don't rock the boat, and don't dare to tread potentially controversial topics like pay raises or higher starting salaries. Agreeing to everything is a sure path to becoming a pushover.

The agreeable employee has a huge workload causing him sleepless nights. He's approached by five colleagues asking for support and agreed to help them all. They've talked, wondering what he does all day if he's got time to help everyone. His boss makes yet another unreasonable demand and he accepts it, disguising his impending doom at how he will get it all done.

Another colleague refuses to help others and when asked the same question demands he is paid more for it and is promoted to a managerial position because he's asked for advice so often. The boss agrees to his demands and delegates some of his workload to the agreeable employee.

Since childhood, most people are told to be kind, put others first, and try to make life run smoothly; the playground peacemaker grows up to be the office diplomat. Being accommodating, agreeable, and selfless actually leads to being undervalued and even excluded from a group. This seems unfair but also likely rings true with experiences you've had in your life.

Clearly there is something else at work behind the compulsion to be agreeable and accommodating. It seems that other people don't always view these traits as positive or pleasurable to be around. When we avoid assertiveness, we don't want to appear rude or selfish, but you're making a bad impression when you appear to be selfless and altruistic. It's in your best interest to assert your rights and boundaries and look after number one.

Choosing and Enforcing Your Boundaries

Being excessively generous, accommodating, and agreeable implies that you would do anything for approval. If you're always willing to do things that others won't, it gives the impression that you have no boundaries. You don't respect yourself enough to draw the line, and thus you find your validation in pleasing others.

In order to protect yourself emotionally, physically, and mentally, you must have limits that stop you from being used, manipulated, or violated. Your boundaries defend your personal space and give you the breathing space you need to ensure you're making decisions based on your own best interests.

There are some common boundaries we all share; no one wants someone to sit on their lap on the subway. The boundaries you choose for yourself will depend on your personality, preferences, beliefs, and needs. In themselves, these boundaries may be changeable: you might set a boundary that says you won't reply to texts after 9:00 p.m. on week nights but will always make yourself available for Skype chats with friends until 2:00 a.m. on weekends.

People are used to the fact you haven't had these boundaries. They rely on having full access to you whenever it suits them. You've been so accommodating historically that they don't need to trouble themselves with whether what they expect from you or how they go about getting it is appropriate. They can justify their behavior with the assumption that if you didn't like it, you would say.

If you're going to enforce boundaries like no longer working unpaid overtime, babysitting on weekends, or lending people money, then you're going to come up against resistance. Choose these limits carefully to ensure the fight is worth it.

Trying to enforce an unrealistic boundary like being undisturbed to practice Pilates everyday between 10:00 and 11:00 a.m. might be impossible if your children or coworkers depend on you being available Monday to Friday at that time.

New people in your life with no preconceptions of you are unlikely to have these negative reactions when you assert your boundaries.

Stating your opinion, asking a question, or acting on your judgement won't make people hate you. They'll accept that you think your table is too cold under the air conditioning, or that they bought out the wrong mains, or that you think you've been waiting too long to be served. They'll still make sure you're sat somewhere else or correct your order; they won't shove a camera in your face and stick your mugshot on their "Not Welcome" board behind the bar.

It's your right to do these things. You may have experienced an upbringing where your boundaries were ignored, perhaps by family members who came into your room without knocking or guilt-tripped you into putting their needs first. You may also have been punished for trying to enforce your boundaries, perhaps by no longer being allowed to use the computer because you didn't let your parents read your private emails.

Despite what you may have learnt, if you healthily assert your boundaries, the disproportionate negative responses you experienced in your upbringing won't appear.

There will of course be times when you get a negative response, are brushed off, or ignored. The liberating realization will be that the positive feeling you get from standing up for yourself in a healthy way beats any negativity thrown at you.

The power of the imagination elevates these situations to soul-crushing nightmares. You'll find that you survive every time you get a negative response; you can brace yourself by accepting you're going to have some brushes with rejection.

Rejection is a flashback of the emotions. It's a titanic force slamming into the child that you once were. Only you're not that child anymore, and this isn't what it was to you then. This is something minor that triggers your body and brain into believing you're in danger.

No matter how helpless you've been, you really do have options now. Other people don't know how hard you're trying and how hard it was for you to say that something wasn't right. When they contradict you, it isn't to deliberately put your body through the trauma you experienced in your upbringing in order to change your mind.

Like mindfulness, these situations are gifts that you can use to explore why some things affect you as much as they do and begin on the path to healing, or at least accepting, those wounds.

Practicing your boundaries with new people is likely to be a positive experience. But you can't hide who you are becoming from the existing people in your life. Anyone who has your best interests at heart should respect you and be proud of your progress.

Healthy relationships, with people who want the best for you, will grow in strength. Those who do become angry or want things to go back to the way they were are doing you a favor because they're identifying themselves as toxic in your life.

Difficult Situations

Once you've chosen not to be a people-pleaser and instead to establish and assert your boundaries, you need to know how to react in a healthy way in challenging situations. Every time this occurs you can gain control of your reaction by asking yourself the following questions:

"Is the situation so distressing that I must address it?"

"Is this going to continue and possibly escalate, or is it one-off?"

"What is going to be lost and what is going to be gained if I pursue this? What are the best- and worst-case scenarios? Is there an outcome where everyone wins?"

"At this point, is it worth using my limited time and energy?"

"Do I have a cutoff point?"

Your cutoff point is when you incur maximum loss, and knowing when this is tells you how long you can stay in a situation before you safely remove yourself from it. You should only be prepared to lose so much before you realize you need to get out.

The power of these questions can be demonstrated by testing them in a difficult situation. You're spending the weekend with relatives, and your aunt greeted you with love but keeps talking about how much you used to sleep in and won't let it drop. She gleefully exclaims that you always were the lazy one when you don't hear someone ask you to pass the salt and your cousin passes it instead.

You know you were a teenager back then and these days you wake early and work hard. It's stopped feeling like a joke and is beginning to feel like a personal attack on you. You use the questions to decide how to react.

The situation is distressing you, but only mildly. The people you keep in touch with know how busy you are and your aunt has always tried to be "the funny one."

This has a small potential to grow, but you rarely see your aunt and so it's unlikely to continue after this night.

You'd win your pride if you addressed this, but you could also upset a lot of people by pursuing it at a family occasion where you suspect no one's taking her seriously.

You find family gatherings stressful and are already using up quite a lot of your reserves. It's going better than expected and you haven't risen to a lot of things you may have a few years ago.

Your cutoff point for family is aggression and violence. Your aunt's attempts at humor are misplaced, but you know she thinks she's being entertaining.

After weighing these questions up, you realize that the night is going better than expected. Your apprehension at the idea of being with family has put you on alert. You realize this may genuinely be your aunt's only memory of you. It's not the worst thing that can happen, and seeing how you so rarely see her, you can have a quick word and hopefully alter her opinion before you all part ways. The thought of confronting her now seems a bit dramatic.

Toxic Takers

The above was a rather mild example of contemplating your boundaries.

Unfortunately, there are many unhealthy people, relationships, and behaviors that don't come from a place of innocence or goodwill. The toxic taker (TT) is a drain who's particularly damaging to unassertive people. It's the TTs who'll be annoyed and upset once you start practicing assertiveness.

There will be people in your life who have a warped sense of entitlement. What you've worked for becomes a free resource they can tap into: they demand a job at your office or introductions to others in your field. They ask you to make them a website for free overnight or use your recruitment knowledge to create their CV.

TTs know your every skill and strength but not a single vulnerability other than your need to say yes: they take from you and return nothing, passing off your work as their own or belittling you to others.

Having grown accustomed to the one-sidedness of the relationship, TTs know how insecure you are so they never consider paying you back or doing something for you. This sends the message that you're less important than them and people are taking advantage of you. The feelings of anger, resentment, and disapproval that arise from this spill over into all areas of your life.

The TT wears many disguises. They could be your colleague, sibling, best friend, neighbor, customer, client, teacher, or acquaintance. The TT needs you to help them—not once or twice, but always. Every encounter involves them sharing with you their latest mistakes, admitting their flaws and weaknesses, and regaling you with tales of the latest disaster that's currently destroying their life.

This is deliberate. Being so open and upfront about their shortcomings endears the TT to you. They ensure there's never time to talk about anything other than themselves and lead you down a path of sob stories and manipulation to get what they want. You're never invited to share your problems but always listen to theirs, go out of your way to help them, and lend them money.

The truth is that the vast majority of TTs actually harbor a lot of resentment for the people they take from. This stems from complex emotions surrounding their dependence on you and resentment that you don't seem to have their worries. They may believe that it's easy for you and you owe it to them to help. You taking an interest in their problems may be the only validation they get.

Even the most independent person falls on hard times and has to ask for help. One of the reasons you might always want to support the TT is because you feel sorry for how often this happens to them. The difference is that things never seem to improve for the TT. If one problem seems to be taken care of, in swoops another one to take its place; the money you lent wasn't enough; the problem was more complex than they first thought. TTs never manage to remove themselves fully from the problematic situation. They're also not afraid to invent disasters in order to extract more from you.

There are two ways to identify and deal with a TT. The first method is that when they come to you with a problem, sympathize with them but don't offer any kind of help at all: no solutions, no money, no advice. Just say, "Yes, that does sound terrible."

This is going to require willpower because the TT will continue to elaborate to provoke your natural caregiving response of wanting to solve the problem. It's hard to listen to their heartbreaking speech and resist the urge to jump in with advice or to be the savior. Just keep sympathizing and stop yourself if you want to say more.

The TT may seem to give up but they're going to try to talk to you again about it. You not offering your usual money or assistance is going to disorient them. When they talk to you, they fully expect you to help them and won't expect you to have seen through their act. You have the power of surprise on your side.

They'll become frustrated and annoyed, but even a TT knows when they're beaten and they'll be off to see who else they can manipulate.

The second method when a TT comes to you with a problem is to sympathize without offering solutions as above, but then tell them a problem of your own.

TTs don't hang around in packs—there's only room for one victim in their life and it's not going to be you. When faced with your problem, they'll appear put out and disinterested. You'll probably enjoy watching their attempts at showing empathy. Having broken the number one rule—that is, TTs come first and you're their personal assistant—they'll regard you as someone who no longer serves a purpose for them.

The speed at which these methods can cause a TT to disappear from your life may surprise you.

When a TT realizes you have your own problems and can't be their constant life support, they'll stop wasting their time on you. If they value the relationship you had, then they may come back, but they may not want a relationship where their crises don't make them special.

Losing a TT is a positive thing, as you'll be able to spend the time you gave them on healthier relationships. The weight and worries of the stress you were carrying for someone else will be gone, too.

Once the initial shock of you not providing a solution or actually having your own problems wears off, you can see what happens after. If the TT loses all interest in you once you stop helping them, you'll know exactly where you stand.

Equipped with the two methods to repel TTs, you can begin to look out for the red flags that let you know who isn't looking for a fair, two-way relationship. There are four common examples of TTs whom you might recognize from your own life.

The first type of TT is the person who won't say hello without an ulterior motive. A colleague who sometimes turns up at your desk with coffee and a smile might baffle you when she blanks you at a social event, until you remember she only ever came to say hi when she needed your help with the printer or some filing.

The second type of TT is the person who won't reciprocate unless forced to. You have lunch with a neighbor once a month and you paid the first time, but then when the bill came at the second lunch, they directed the waiter to you and you paid again. You meet for this month's lunch and find you've forgotten your wallet. Your neighbor pays, but you can tell they're not happy about it. When you go to pencil next month's date in your diary, they tell you they're actually pretty booked up for the rest of the year.

The third type of TT is the person who requires a payment or quid pro quo for them to help you. You ask your new partner to pick up some onions on the way to your apartment for the meal you're making and they ask you to transfer them the money. You laugh, assuming they're joking, but when they arrive they ask you for the exact change. When you needed them to pick you up on their way home and drop you along their normal route, they asked you for gas money as if they were going out of their way.

The fourth type of TT is the person who doesn't ask about you or really care. You could recite your best friend's birthday, recent weight gain, bank balance, latest disappointment, and enemies. When they invite you over on a Tuesday, you're surprised as they know you have evening classes—at least you thought they did, until they innocently say, "An evening class? That doesn't sound like you. Why are you starting that?" You spill your heart out about a problem you haven't been able to share with anyone else and you look over and see them smiling at their phone. They notice you looking and say, "That sounds great. Well done, you."

TTs are tiring and always want more. They don't like boundaries and they certainly don't like assertiveness. They have a great eye for identifying accommodating and agreeable people who don't know their rights. TTs prey on generous people-pleasers and won't stop taking until their victim either stops offering solutions or wants to talk about their own problems.

Although they must be condemned for taking advantage of your weakness, TTs do serve a purpose in highlighting how your people-pleasing compulsions aren't respected or deserved by others.

If you feel any hint of people-pleasing habits, you must be aware of what can lie in your path. You've read about manipulating behavior, people who will repeatedly violate your boundaries, and even TTs who are out to get you. Even if you are assertive, it doesn't mean you are immunized from these people. You can begin to understand that there is more than meets the eye to being "nice" and agreeable and realize even more why assertiveness is an essential life skill.

Takeaways:

1. We tend to think being agreeable and accommodating are positive traits. They are, but selectively so. Studies have shown that too much of either conveys a negative impression to others—precisely what you want to prevent by not asserting yourself. Thus, it seems to make more sense to assert yourself on a consistent basis and stop the need for people-pleasing.

2. Boundaries become important very quickly to enforce, both to assert your rights and to defend against those who would seek to take advantage of you. TTs are the epitome of those who would seek to take advantage of you, and they come in many forms of selfishness and non-reciprocation.

3. People-pleasing ends when you start to take control of difficult situations and, essentially, become comfortable with confrontation. This is dictated by your cutoff point, which is the point at which you must act.

Chapter 7. The Instinct to Apologize

Do you find yourself apologizing often, even in situations most people would think unnecessary? Does the word "sorry" live on the tip of your tongue? Do you utter it frequently, even when you've done nothing wrong?

Many of us over-apologize as an instinct. As a child, you might have learned to avoid conflict or were expected to take someone else's blame. Maybe your parents taught you that it was polite, or they expected you to own up to your mistakes.

The word "sorry" has become something we reactively utter. Whether or not they actually commit an offense, it just slips out. Though it seems like a harmless habit, it can actually lower your self-esteem, justify and reinforce others' poor actions, and potentially turn you into a pushover. There's no shame in apologizing for a mistake or wrongdoing. But what happens when saying sorry becomes an automatic response to anything that makes you feel even slightly uncomfortable?

You might apologize when *someone else* bumps into you at a bar or club. You put your hands up and smile to show that no harm was done and find yourself scrambling to say "sorry." Even though the other person spilled half of your expensive drink on the floor and *you don't actually feel sorry*, it seems like the appropriate response. As you imagine this situation, ask yourself if it was courteous to do that. Which result did you want to achieve by using that word? The compulsive "sorry" that escaped your mouth probably *wasn't* an apology. It was just a way to avoid confrontation and a possibly awkward situation.

By "apologizing" like this, you tell others *you are taking responsibility* for the issue. That person at the bar may now assume it was *your* fault that the spilled drink almost came into contact with their new pair of shoes. In trivial situations such as this one, it doesn't really matter who was at fault. But when over-apologizing becomes a habit, there is an increased likelihood of it occurring in situations that *do* matter. You can imagine how this affects your assertiveness.

What Does "Sorry" Say?

Unnecessary apologies can send the message that you'd rather be agreeable than honest and rather make excuses than assert yourself. Doing so frequently could make you come across as submissive or a pushover. This could make you a potential target for being taken advantage of at work and at home.

Over-apologizing also creates an unnecessary sense of guilt and can undermine your own self-worth. When apologizing becomes second nature to you, not only do you remind others that you're responsible for what goes wrong, you're also directing that information to yourself. It's like volunteering to be the scapegoat and even trying to get others to reinforce it as fact. The cycle continues when you start feeling worse and people blame you even more.

Before you start to apologize, stop and ask yourself two questions:

• *"Did I actually do something wrong?"*
• And if not, *"Did I really want to communicate that I think I did?"*

Apologizing could also be the result of a genuine desire to demonstrate respect. It becomes a problem, though, when holding others' opinions or reactions in overly high regard. One thing to remember is that we are all human, and we don't have to put any one person or ideal on a pedestal. Those well-intended attempts at politeness can sabotage us years later by turning into a people-pleasing addiction.

A tendency to over-apologize may also stem from an aversion to conflict. People turn to it as a means of claiming responsibility in hopes of making a problem disappear. This "preemptive" peacekeeping strategy—regardless of whether or not you are to blame—can wreak havoc on your self-image. At home or in the workplace, you could be making yourself look incompetent or even annoy those around you with regular negativity and self-deprecation.

Imagine a situation in which you would have to confront an overbearing or highly critical boss. You become nervous as you get closer to his office. When you enter, you see that he's just getting off the phone. As he hangs up, he looks up at you and asks, "What?" As you scramble for the right words, the word "sorry" naturally jumps off your tongue. By the time you get your sentences straight, the conversation is over and you realize that half of your sentences were made up by this apologetic word. Maybe you were trying to protect yourself from rejection. Perhaps you were intimidated by his blunt speaking style. Whatever the case, your request probably wasn't fulfilled because saying *sorry* got in the way.

Men and Women

According to a 2010 study in the journal *Psychological Science,* "women have a lower threshold for what constitutes offensive behavior" and are likelier to see a need to apologize in everyday situations. In comparison, men are less likely to see fault in their own behavior and do not feel the need to apologize as often. This difference might be due to socialization. For example, "boys will be boys" is often be a phrase used to excuse bad behavior—without an apology. The paradox is that the same isn't usually applicable to girls.

Generally speaking, girls are generally raised to be peacekeepers or to be "pleasant." On the other hand, boys are oftentimes not held to the same expectations. This could be among many reasons why women are more likely to blame themselves in an argument than men, for example.

Sometimes, we'll throw an apology into situations where directness and confidence are key, such as asking for a raise. What kind of impression do you give others when you start a sentence with "sorry"? Here are some examples:

Sorry, I didn't want to interrupt, but . . .
I'm sorry, I didn't want to bother you, but would you mind . . .
Sorry, could I ask you a favor . . .

Phrases like these litter our speech, and each time we use them, we weaken our own voices. There is no need to be afraid of rejection or being called a jerk. Go ahead and say what you mean and ask for what you want. You don't have to apologize for it, nor do you need to water it down. If you're new to this, you might get mixed reactions. It might make others confused or even angry at first. Don't worry about this. When you say what you mean, people will learn to hear you out. They'll soon begin to understand and respect you.

Once again, starting out or even greeting someone with "sorry" can make you look bad. If you want to make a good impression, such as when requesting a promotion or closing a sale, ask yourself how confident you would appear if you saw yourself from someone else's shoes. Would you give yourself the promotion? Would you buy something from a salesperson who asked, "Sorry, but could I interest you in maybe buying something?"

When you need to make a serious statement, nothing takes away the gravity behind your words faster than saying, "I'm sorry." An apology can make demands sound like requests. Don't be alarmed if you find yourself deflating your sentences like this. Just realize that you are not communicating as clearly as you could. Take these two examples:

I'm sorry, but I think maybe we'd all be a little more comfortable if you wouldn't make sexist jokes about the new intern. Is that okay? I don't want to step on your toes . . .

Does that seem like a demand or an option to you? Don't be surprised if people mistake it for the latter. The hedging flows effortlessly after opening with an apology, and often the impact will be lost completely.

Your sexist jokes need to stop.

This is a powerful statement—one that calls for a response. Try it out yourself and watch how reactions change. This is assertiveness, and you can see how easily it springs from simply altering your vocabulary.

Forget Your Past

Many people allow themselves to become products of their experiences. Though our experiences help shape who we are and in which direction we grow, we can also develop habits like over-apologizing. This could be in reaction to a buildup of bad past experiences.

You may want to ask yourself a few of the following questions:

- *What's the first reaction you have when someone tells you no?*
  Are you afraid of rejection? Do you immediately feel discouraged when you hear no? Whenever you talk to someone, you risk being rejected or criticized. But it's even riskier trying to avoid rejection or criticism completely, because you'll never give yourself the chance to understand what someone means. No could mean "no, not right now, but later yes," or "no, not this, but something similar could be a solution."

- *Was advocating on your own behalf off-limits in your family? Was it encouraged?*
  If you got into an argument with a parent or sibling, were you allowed to talk back, or did you have to hold it in? Maybe you had to live with someone who always had

to be right. Perhaps you had insensitive family members who refused to apologize about anything. Your apologetic reactions could be "making up" for their sense of pride.

- *When you were younger, was it acceptable to speak up and share your opinion?*
  Growing up, were your views taken seriously? Perhaps your parents or older siblings talked down to you and minimized what you had to say. Now, you find yourself downplaying your own thoughts and even apologize for coming up with an idea or suggestion.

- *What other major experiences shaped your outlook regarding asserting yourself and respecting authority, particularly at the workplace?*
  Do you find yourself intimidated by a particular manager or coworker? You probably had a parent or other family member with a strong personality. Now, you find it difficult to assert yourself or make requests around such people, as

they may remind you of the personality types that were present in your childhood.

Next, examine the contexts in which your "sorry" impulse comes out.

Start to identify triggers that exacerbate the behavior such as certain people, contexts, moods, or times of the day. For example, you might find that you are likelier to say sorry when you are tired. If you don't get enough sleep, or are lacking energy after lunch, it might just be easier to apologize than to explain yourself or argue your point of view.

Also, pay attention to whether your tendency to over-apologize comes out with some people more than others. For instance, a pushy, demanding client who constantly requests impossible deadlines may send your stress (and your "sorry" reflex) into overdrive. Once again, try to see if such personality types resemble anyone from your childhood. If your client reminds you of your older sister who constantly rushed you and always looked over your shoulder, you'll be able to make the connection between your reactions and your history. You can then catch yourself mid-habit and eventually stop it.

Don't Apologize; Be Accurate

At first this can be a tricky. There's no shame in asking for verbal do-overs, especially with family and friends. For example, if you need to cancel happy hour plans with a friend and find yourself apologizing out of habit, catch yourself and say, "You know, what I really wanted to say is . . ." or "Thanks a lot for understanding. It's a crazy week with all these upcoming deadlines and I appreciate you being flexible." That's it. How does that compare to saying, "Sorry, sorry, I'm the worst, I know"?

You can accomplish clearer and more accurate communication by simply changing your vocabulary. When you identify who or what makes you apologize most, you can turn awkward moments into a trigger point for your new phrases. For example, after becoming aware of your habit, you might switch from saying *sorry* about bumping into others to *excuse me*. You can still be nice without subjecting yourself to blame upfront.

Avoiding Conflict

Over-apologizing is often a side effect of a conflict-avoidance pattern that has been hardwired over time.

If you were raised in an abusive family or felt you had to hide your ideas or the way you are, you probably grew tired from the consequences of disapproval. Learning to avoid confrontation then came naturally as a way of coping. Although you might think that you're getting around conflict, you really aren't. We'll often say yes when we mean no because we don't trust that someone making a request can cope with rejection. It's easy to avoid your true feelings, especially if you have difficulty doing well under pressure, don't have emotional stability, or tend to over-dramatize how a discussion or argument will go before it happens.

For example, a coworker might ask you if you want to switch shifts. Depending on which coworker it is, it might be harder or easier to say no. If the coworker seems excited and very sure that you'll take the shift, it may be difficult to say no or to say no without saying sorry. You could even subscribe to her request out loud but regret your words deep down.

Part of becoming more assertive is getting better at dealing with conflict. Every confrontation might feel like a miniature conflict—big and scary when you're first thrown into it. But once you start to ask questions and gather more information, not only will tense situations be diffused, but you may also even come to an agreement or find out where there might have been a misunderstanding.

Discover what people really want. Once, there were two people fighting over an orange. Each one wanted it in its entirety. But when asked why they want the whole orange, one replied, "I need all the juice to make my cake." The other said, "I need all the zest from the peel to make my frosting." What seems to be a conflict may not even be a conflict at all. Just because someone says they want something doesn't mean that you have a full understanding of their goals.

Dig a little deeper for more information. Neutral questions like "Tell me a bit more about how you envision this" or "Help me understand where you're coming from" will often reveal an easy win-win.

Assume flexibility. Just because someone is enthusiastic, or even firm about something, doesn't necessarily mean that they've closed off all suggestions. I have this problem a lot. I'll get so excited about something and then talk a mile a minute. People often assume that I'm unwilling to consider anything different. Confronting a dominant personality doesn't have to be combative.

Simply ask, "Are you open for feedback on this?" If they say yes, which most people will, you can start by saying, "I tend to think of these things from a different perspective." It keeps the conversation neutral. You're not attacking their point of view. Instead, you're just sharing yours. High-energy people move quickly and enthusiastically. They may even end up loving your idea and embracing it with the same zeal they do their own.

Determine if your ego is being bruised or something else. To avoid lingering resentments and dirty looks, you must give up your goal of crushing the competition. Any loudmouth can "win" an argument. To be a true winner, your aim should be a win-win for everyone. If you hear yourself saying things like "Technically, you never said that" or find yourself plotting to secretly tape the person so you can prove you're right, both of you have already lost.

Stick to the facts. Facts are neither incendiary nor insulting. They are objective. To an adolescent, for example, you could say, "I notice the clean laundry is in a pile on your floor. And it's Friday, which is allowance day."

Let her make the connection. Hopefully, you won't need to say another word. My favorite example of this technique comes from a friend who recently returned from a military deployment.

Instead of scolding a reporter about how his shirt would give away their position, he simply said, "That's a really bright shirt." You can say more with less simply by sticking to what's important.

When and How to Apologize Effectively

If you find that over-apologizing is a regular thing for you, do not despair. You don't have to become a mean or hard person to change this. You also don't have to give up apologizing completely. There are indeed instances where a proper apology is appropriate. However, always being sorry, or frequently apologizing, to the point that it damages your self-esteem or makes you afraid to confront others is problematic. Confident, assertive people are self-aware and are neither afraid to admit their mistakes nor willing to shut themselves down before making a statement.

To ensure that you aren't compromising your self-esteem or putting yourself in a bad position, here's what you should not include in an apology:

- *Don't make promises you can't keep.*

    You shouldn't tell someone "This will never happen again" if it's not 100% in your control. If you make a promise that you end up breaking later on, you will lose credibility (possibly leading to even more apologies).

- *Don't defend yourself by blaming someone else or minimizing the problem.*

    Putting the problem on someone else or making it seem smaller than it is will make your apology less effective. It might seem insincere or look like you are trying to avoid blame. Don't be afraid to own up to your mistakes. This, however, doesn't mean that you need to put yourself down.

- *Don't over-apologize.*

  The word "sorry" will lose all meaning if you say it too often. Others may interpret it as just a way to get out of a discussion or that you are just a pleaser and not a genuine person.

Dr. Beth Polin, an assistant professor of management at Eastern Kentucky University and coauthor of *The Art of the Apology*, defines an apology as a statement that includes one or more of six components:

- An expression of regret: This is the actual "I'm sorry" statement.

- An explanation: This is a clarification of what happened, not a justification.

- An acknowledgment of responsibility: In other words, owning up to your mistakes.

- A declaration of repentance: For example, "I truly regret what I did."

- An offer of repair: "Maybe I can turn this around."

- A request for forgiveness: "I know I messed up, but I'm truly sorry and I'm asking your forgiveness."

Apologies play an important role in any type of relationship. If one party makes a mistake or causes another pain, saying sorry may not only be polite, but sometimes it's necessary. However, no single person is wrong all the time. It simply isn't accurate to feel the need to apologize for every little thing, even the ones for which you were not at fault. As we discussed, over-apology usually turns out to be anything but an apology. It's often a defense mechanism, whether for the sake of preemptive "peacekeeping" or fearing confrontation. In the journey to become more confident and assertive, saying sorry too much can really stunt your progress. It can also affect your communication by making it unclear to others what you really want or need. Once you recognize and tackle this pattern, you may start to see your life and interactions with others improve.

Overall, the urge and instinct to apologize is something that becomes hardwired over time as a natural instinct to avoid confrontation and displeasure. Of course, it is the absolute contrary feeling to assertiveness, where you are rather making waves and withstanding tension as opposed to running from it.

Takeaways:

1. Apologizing is the opposite of assertiveness—at least when you do it out of instinct like many of us are prone to do. Over-apologizing, however, does give a peek into how you view yourself and the patterns you've been exposed to. We are all products of our past experiences, and many have told us that apologies and not making waves is the best way to get through life unscathed.

2. Men and women have markedly different approaches to over-apologizing, just like how they tend to be different in terms of assertiveness. It is mostly socialization and gender roles.

3. Another reason for the instinct to apologize is to avoid conflict. Conflict is tense and uncomfortable, but it is the essence of assertiveness. Becoming

comfortable with it by changing your vocabulary to apologize less is an important step.

4. How do you apologize when you actually should? Include one of six elements articulated by Beth Polin and make sure to actually take responsibility and not deflect or blame others.

Chapter 8. Understanding Your Patterns

Everyone's unique, but understanding which category most represents you in certain areas will highlight your strengths and weaknesses surrounding asserting yourself. Your communication style is how you interact with and relate to others and how you feel most confident dealing with them. It's normal to have a default style but behave differently with different people or in different circumstances.

Psychotherapist Carl Benedict has written about four communication styles and how they relate to assertiveness. In order to know yourself, you've got to be able to identify how the messages you send yourself determine the impression others get of you. Seeing the gaps in your thinking will show you where you can add steps into your behavior that will allow you to communicate assertively.

Passive Communication Style

Passive communication occurs in people with low self-esteem who feel they can't control themselves or others. They believe they're not worth having their needs met and so avoid expressing any desires or opinions and won't stand up for themselves.

This avoidant behavior means they never confront painful or upsetting situations. Instead, they stew on the issue and allow their anger to boil right up to their high level of tolerance for unfair situations until eventually they explode. Allowing their resentment to build for so long means that their reaction is not in proportion to the original perceived slight. This outburst leaves them feeling guilty and, not believing they have the right to ask anything of others, they revert back to being passive.

Passive communicators tend to give weak eye contact and talk in an apologetic tone. They slump their body, trying to be as unnoticed as their needs and opinions. They develop anxiety from feelings of lack of control and suffer from depression. They genuinely don't understand their needs, have low self-worth, and wish someone would think of their feelings for once.

An employee brings in milk every week and labels it as hers before putting it into the work fridge. Every few days she finds it slightly less full than when she left it, and one day she catches her colleague using it. The colleague laughs and says, "Busted! I only use a bit anyway," and walks off. Furious but unable to say anything, the employee stews for days until she finally loses her temper and dumps a carton of milk over her colleague's head, screaming at her for being selfish. She feels so guilty afterward that, despite getting off with just a warning, she resigns, unable to face her colleague again.

You can see how the employee's passive communication style didn't allow her to be assertive. Rather than pretending not to notice or that everything's fine, she had the right to tell the colleague not to use anything of hers. Her inability to control her boiled-over temper led to more unassertive behavior where she didn't respect the rights of her colleague. Her lack of self-compassion stopped her from forgiving herself and she had to leave her job.

Aggressive Communication Style

Aggressive communication is the passive communicator at their worst, but all the time. Aggressive communicators put their needs, rights, and self-expression before others. They use verbal and physical violence and aggression to violate the rights of others in their need for self-satisfaction. This style is often the result of their own mistreatment in the past at the hands of others, which caused low self-esteem and emotional pain.

The stance of an aggressive communicator is overbearing and they often give intense eye contact. Their voice matches their posture and is loud and challenging.

They're impulsive, poor listeners who interrupt and try to dominate others. They criticize, humiliate, and are quick to blame anything and everything on whoever's in the firing line. Naturally, this behavior generates extremely negative responses in people who interact with them, including hatred, avoidance, fear, and alienation.

A man goes to a bar and tells the barman to turn off the TV and put music on. The barman politely tells him when the game will finish and says that, as they're a sports bar, he can't turn it off. The man loses his temper and threatens the barman, who calls security and promptly serves him a ban for life. The aggressive man is quickly running out of places he's allowed to enter.

It wasn't assertive of the man to put his own needs in front of everyone else's. He lost self-control when he was unable to control others, and his aggression was disproportionate. If he had been assertive, he would have realized it was the right of the venue to decide whether to show sports or not and he can please himself better by going elsewhere. Instead, his aggression ruined the evening for the barman, patrons, and himself and could have resulted in a criminal record.

Although opposite, both passive and aggressive communicators are unable to grow and mature because problems are never dealt with in a healthy and effective way.

Passive-Aggressive Communication Style

Passive-aggressive communication is a combination of the above behaviors. These people appear passive but act out their aggression through covert, indirect acts of anger. This style comes from feelings of powerlessness and the inability to face the actual problematic person or situation. Instead, they choose to retaliate indirectly by appearing fine on the surface but undermining those who they feel have wronged them.

Passive-aggressive communicators often use sarcasm and inappropriate emotions, smiling even when something has angered them, and mutter under their breath instead of speaking out.

Their preferred weapons of revenge are sabotage after assuring those involved that they're fine. Appearing cooperative, they quietly cause disruption. They alienate themselves and fail to establish any real power because they give the appearance of not having a problem with the actual issue at hand. This prevents them from growing.

A busy receptionist receives a reprimand from his boss for leaving dirty water jugs and glasses in the meeting room. He apologizes to his boss's face but curses him when his back is turned. Noticing that the ink is running low, he declines to tell his boss, even though he knows that he has to print 20 reports for the meeting the next day. He receives an urgent message and writes it on a Post-it, which he slips into the boss's overstuffed pigeon hole rather than pass it on in person. The dirty glasses go straight back in the cupboard instead of the dishwasher.

The receptionist was at fault and should have accepted his own mistake. If his boss had been aggressive toward him, he would have had a reason to stand up for himself by asserting how he expected to be spoken to professionally. He put his need for revenge above the needs of his colleagues and set himself up for further reprimands down the line. If he had been assertive, he may have been able to delegate some tasks from his workload in order to give himself more time.

Assertive Communication Style

Assertive communication is standing up for yourself, being clear and direct when sharing your thoughts and feelings, and protecting your rights without taking away the rights of other people. Assertive communication is a product of high self-esteem and doesn't come naturally to people who haven't been taught to respect themselves and others and to value themselves on a physical, spiritual, and emotional level.

Assertive communicators are just as good at listening as they are at clearly making their point. They don't allow others to abuse them and make sure to treat others respectfully, giving good eye contact and standing tall with open, relaxed body language. They feel they deserve a fair outcome and are confident in themselves, creating a safe platform for others to express their views. They feel connected to the world around them, and all challenges are seen as an opportunity to mature.

People respond well to assertive communicators, as they feel respected and know they aren't expected to provide anything they didn't agree to. They know the assertive communicator will have well thought-out reasons for making their point and are inclined to treat them fairly in response.

Assertive communicators can navigate any situation without the hangover of resentment, anger, or lack of control that the other three styles generate. The assertive communicator doesn't dread confrontation or overcompensate for feelings of insecurity by bullying others. They ask for their needs to be met and accept the response; in turn, they expect others to respect them when they give their own opinion.

An angry customer has raised his voice at a retail worker who calmly explains that although she understands he's angry, she doesn't deserve to be spoken to in that way at work and is doing her best but can't help him if he continues. Her active listening and reasonable request placates the customer, who apologizes, explains he is stressed because the item he is looking for is a last-minute birthday gift, and gratefully accepts her help to find a suitable substitute.

This communication style lends itself perfectly to being assertive, as she was able to look after her own rights while finding a win-win solution. She wasn't passive by accepting the man's bad behavior or aggression by losing her temper so she didn't compromise her own needs. Giving the customer an option to change his tone or leave the store rather than trying to control him further confirmed her assertive style and led to the best possible outcome.

Choosing to Be Assertive

You can identify which of the four communication styles you've adopted in any situation by noticing the types of phrases you're using.

The passive communicator says, "People walk all over me" and "No one cares how I feel about this."

The aggressive communicator says, "I always get what I want—whatever it takes" and "You're worthless; you owe me."

The passive-aggressive communicator says, "That's fine . . . (That's what you think)" and "They'll see what happens to people who cross me."

The assertive communicator says, "We're both entitled to respectfully express our opinion" and "I'm responsible for myself and no one owes me anything."

Passive people suffer because they feel they have no control over other people. They don't have the confidence to stand up for themselves or even add their opinion to the discussion, so they also lose all feelings of having control over themselves.

Aggressive people have control over themselves and feel they should also be able to control others. Using fear and bullying to subdue and dominate does work but only in the short term. People go to great lengths to escape an aggressive person, and it only takes a small interaction for people to decide they'll actively avoid them.

Assertiveness prevents these control traps, but you may still worry that being more assertive to achieve your goals could cause you to act badly. Randy J. Peterson, Professor of Psychology and Psychiatry at the University of British Columbia, said there is a simple way to determine whether or not you are being assertive: if your intention is to have control of your own actions, you're being assertive; if your intention is to have control of someone else, you're being aggressive.

If you feel completely out of control, you're being passive.

Forgetting that you are in control of yourself leads to the feelings of helplessness that drive passive behavior. A passive communicator will let others weaken or spoil what they try to do or allow them to make decisions on their behalf. Anger at how their passivity has caused people to treat them can turn into retaliation in the form of aggression, where they try to dominate others, or passive-aggressive behavior, where they stay weak but punish behind the scenes.

It's normal to want to have command of yourself, and being assertive means acknowledging what you want while understanding no one's under any obligation to provide it for you.

Passive people forget that they have a choice, but they have actually been making choices the whole time: it's a choice to do nothing. It's a choice to not speak up, to allow someone to bully you, and be forced into something you don't want. The passive employee tells themselves they have to do what their boss says, but the truth is that they don't, not really. Other people say no and they aren't fired and blacklisted and run out of town.

Passive people don't have perspective on the consequences of saying no. They assume it's a deal breaker, a sure-fire way to destroy a relationship in one deadly word. People say no all the time without their whole world tumbling down around them.

Questioning what you want and determining if it's about controlling yourself or controlling others can help you stay committed to behaving assertively. You don't have to agree with or even understand another's reasons and views to be able to respect that they have them. You can listen to their needs and decide for yourself whether or not you can assist them without having to devalue what they desire. There will be situations where you choose to go along with something that might inconvenience you, but it was your freedom of choice to decide to do so.

There are some things you can try today that will take you to the realm of the assertive style of communication. Using "I" statements when speaking up for yourself stops you from placing blame on others or trying to control them and keeps your focus on you. It's assertive to say you disagree, but if that seems like a huge deal, start by refusing to let yourself give in and instead practice saying, "Let me think about that and get back to you." When you feel more confident, you can assertively say no. It's fine to be a broken record if people won't accept the answer you're giving it—just keep asserting yourself in the same way without worrying over excuses or justifications.

Self-Assessment

Finding out your communication style may confirm your suspicions or be a complete surprise. This self-assessment, like the one by performance communication expert Amy Castro, will give you vital insight into how your type is determining your life.

Make a note of your answers to the following questions. Once completed, add up the A's, B's, C's, and D's and then check your results with the answers at the end of the quiz.

1) Someone pushes in front of you in the queue for train tickets and you're running late. You're likely to say:
   a) Nothing at all, as you don't want to start a scene.
   b) "Have I been standing here so long I've turned into a ghost? Can you not see me?"
   c) "Get to the back of this line now and wait your turn!"
   d) "Oh, excuse me, I'm actually waiting this queue."
2) The grass on your lawn is overgrown and you need to mow. As you go outside you're likely to say:
   a) "This grass has got so long. I hope I have time to cut it before that storm they forecasted starts."
   b) "Wow, imagine what it would be like if somebody actually helped me for once."
   c) "Stop being so lazy and get out here now to help!"
   d) "I'd like some help outside. Please could you rake after I've mowed?"

3) You're in a busy shoe shop and ask the assistant to bring you a pair of trainers in a size four. They return and hand you a box that says size four on it, but inside the trains are a size 11. You're likely to say:

    a) "I must have said the wrong size. I'll be able to get an idea if I try these ones on."

    b) "Do I look like a clown or do you always recommend wearing shoes twice the size of your feet?"

    c) "Get the manager now. This is terrible service and you're awful at your job!"

    d) "There's been a mistake. Could you see if there are any fours out back please?"

4) Your book group is discussing what to read for next month's meeting. They're considering the latest horror, but you've heard it's really gory and you hate anything scary. You're likely to say:

    a) "You all have great taste in books. I'm happy if you are."

b) "Great, so I'm in a book club full of serial killers. How about a book that isn't for the criminally insane?"

c) "You're stupid if you think I'll read this and none of you should either!"

d) "I've heard there's a lot of gore and I find that really unpleasant to read."

5) You're looking forward to going for a meal with friends. Your parent calls and asks for your help putting some boxes up in the attic. You're likely to say:

a) "Erm . . . Okay, I'm on my way. I better get off the phone. I need to make a call."

b) "Does my number only appear in your contacts list when you need something? Call someone who doesn't have a life."

c) "I don't know why you think I'm your servant, but you should call someone who has time for this!"

d) "I'm just on my way for a few drinks, but I'll come over on the way home."

6) You overhear a member of your evening class say they don't like you because you ask too many questions. You're most likely to say:

    a) Nothing. You're humiliated and upset and stay silent in class.

    b) "Professor, I've got a few questions that I think will really benefit the class . . . About six, actually."

    c) "Why don't you say that again to my face?"

    d) "I overheard you earlier and now that I've got you alone. I was wondering if we could talk about it?"

7) You're having problems at work with a temp who keeps turning up late. Your boss pulls you aside and asks what you think. You're most likely to say:

    a) "I'm not sure. What are you thinking?"

    b) "What genius hired them anyway? Oh yeah, it was Debbie, the queen of bad decisions."

    c) "All temps are awful. That's why they can't get real jobs."

d) "We should talk to the agency about getting someone more reliable."

8) Five of you are at a diner and you go up to the counter and order five hotdogs. The server mishears you and brings out nine. You're most likely to say:

a) "Sorry, guys, it must have been my fault. I'll pay for the extras."

b) "Five doesn't sound remotely close to nine—I guess they don't pay you to think."

c) "I'm not paying for something I didn't order so get your manager here now!"

d) "I ordered five. Could you take these extra ones back please?"

9) You're late for the school run and your neighbor grabs you on the way to your car for a chat about her new wine tasting class. You're most likely to say:

a) "That sounds great. Yes, I'd love to hear all about it."

b) "Have you seen what time it is, or have you started your wine tasting this morning?"

c) "I don't care about your pathetic little hobby. Move out of my way!"

d) "It sounds like you'll have a great time. I'm late to drop the kids off so I have to get going."

10) You're meeting a friend to see a movie they've chosen that you've heard awful reviews of from everyone who's seen it. You're most likely to say:

a) "What did you think? Me too."

b) "Well you've got bad taste in hair and clothes so why should I have expected any different from your choice of films?"

c) "It was the worst film ever and you're stupid for thinking it wouldn't be!"

d) "I did know the reviews were bad— I should have shown you them before."

11) You forgot to cancel a subscription for your partner and they're angry that the money has come out of their bank so they loudly confront you. You're most likely to say:

a) "You never do anything. You be in charge of everything from now on then instead of me."

b) "Says Mr. Perfect who never makes any mistakes, except for basically every decision you ever make."

c) "Sorry, you're right!"

d) "I forgot to cancel it. You're right. I'd appreciate if you could talk to me about this rather than shout at me."

Total number of A's:

Total number of B's:

Total number of C's:

Total number of D's:

If you have two similar high scores, this indicates you use both, but the higher communication style score tends to be the one you go to first.

Mostly A's: Your Communication Style is Passive

If you got mostly A's, this result is more like your lack-of-communication style. You're probably seen as agreeable and accommodating by those in your life and you attract people who like you because you don't ask for anything and always say yes. It's unlikely your needs are met, and these same people probably take advantage of you. Your inability to express yourself causes frustration that manifests as physical symptoms of stress and ill bodily and mental health.

You're too focused on other people's needs and need to practice being assertive to get your own needs met. A positive approach to yourself and the situations you find yourself in is key to assertive behavior, and you will find that you're happier and start earning real respect.

Mostly B's: Your Communication Style is Passive-Aggressive

It's likely if you got mostly B's that you were once taught that expressing yourself led to ridicule or invalidation. You've learnt that although you can't express yourself honestly, you can use sarcasm to say what you want, safe in the knowledge that you can fall back on the excuse that you were just joking.

There's nothing funny about this communication style when you consider it's the most damaging of all four, combining the worst bits of passive and aggressive behavior. It confuses people dealing with you, who also find that any attempts at understanding the real issue are rejected or twisted.

Although passive-aggression can be passed off as humor, it's actually a blow to the self-esteem of the people on the receiving end. It's a huge wall to honest communication that could bring about real change, and the longer the defense is up, the harder it is to be candid and real about your needs to yourself and others.

Despite your past experiences of expressing yourself, it's never too late to change, and your current communication style is directly working against you. An honest approach is key to assertive behavior that will bring you happiness and respect.

Mostly C's: Your Communication Style is Aggressive

A result of mostly C's means you operate using tactics like intimidation, expressing your negative opinion as fact, and being overbearing; it works and people usually do what you say. You consider this communication style to be honest and people always know exactly where you stand, but it isn't without its casualties.

You might get short-term obedience, but over time you will realize that most of your employees don't last longer than a few months, any acquaintances you have soon stop answering your calls, and customers or people who need your help take their business or curiosity elsewhere.

You often focus too much on your own needs, and the constant confrontation to fight unworthy battles means the consequences far outweigh any benefit. Refraining from trying to control others and remembering they deserve the respect you demand from them will help you behave in an assertive way. This will bring happiness to your life.

Mostly D's: Your Communication Style is Assertive

Scoring mostly D's is the healthiest, most positive result you can get and the communication style most suitable to allowing you to control your own destiny and meet your needs. You stand up for yourself but care for others, too, respecting them in the same way you expect to be respected. You're likely to have strong relationships and use your abilities to enable positive solutions for everyone.

Your calm and approachable presence puts people at ease, and you are unlikely to receive the negative responses that people without your communication skills have to endure. This isn't to say you don't have to work at this style. Unless you scored all D's, you may revert to less positive communication styles when in stressful situations. It's worth understanding these elements of yourself so you can continue to grow and improve your assertiveness.

Developing Your Communication Style

Contrasting your results with your real-life behaviors can shine a light on whether you are who you think you are. This objective view provides an insight into how others view you and whether you've been acting against your own interests.

Whichever of the four communication styles you are most like or whether you are a combination of them all, it directly contributes to how others negotiate with you.

Your passiveness could be leading them to assume you actually like it when people decide for you. Your aggression may have scared people into avoiding you at all costs. Examples of your passive-aggressive behavior might have given you the reputation of a fake snake in the grass.

Whether intentional or not, your communication style affects your relationships and interactions and ultimately your ability to be assertive. Understanding your communication style prevents the damage caused by you subconsciously sabotaging your attempts.

Takeaways:

1. There are generally four styles of communication: passive, aggressive, passive-aggressive, and assertive. You can guess which one is the best to shoot for.
2. Assertive communication is standing up for yourself, being clear and direct when sharing your thoughts and feelings, and protecting your rights without taking away the rights of other people. Assertive communication is a product of high self-esteem and doesn't come naturally to people who haven't been taught to respect themselves and others and to value themselves on a physical, spiritual, and emotional level.

Chapter 9. Assertiveness Action Plan

Armed with the theories, research, and a new understanding of what contributes to assertiveness, you can confidently begin practicing in your own life. Raising your confidence and self-worth will lower your need to be a people-pleaser and the respect you get and give yourself will spur you on. It won't happen overnight and it will require hard work, but if you commit to doing as much as you can, you'll see positive life-changing results.

Phase 1

This beginning phase is about practicing assertiveness safely in your mind, alone, and in situations that don't frighten you. It will ease you in to the work you'll be doing over the next three weeks and will help you come to terms with your own behavior and how you can become more assertive. All you need is a pen and paper or a computer and to be kind to and accepting of yourself.

Day 1

Reflect on situations mentioned in the book or times when you have felt unassertive and write down what happened. You don't need to think about how you reacted yet; just get a good list of at least five scenarios where you were walked all over, ignored, manipulated and disrespected, and/or when you acted in this way.

For example:

1) My colleague smirked when I said something in a meeting and talked over me.

2) My neighbor always guilt-trips me into clearing her garden but never helps with mine.
3) I don't tell my partner I'm upset with them.
4) I deserve a pay rise but three years later I'm still on a starter's salary.
5) My best friend tries to bring up the problems I'm having.

Day 2

Take your list and write down how you reacted. Again, don't judge yourself or worry that you have far too much work to do to even begin. This is about accepting where you are—the only way from here is up.

For example:

1) I didn't say anything to my colleague but I cried in the toilets.
2) I just do what she says and go home exhausted and annoyed at myself.
3) I blank them and deliberately sabotage plans.

4) I just look at my friends' social media and resent the things they can buy with their money.
5) I mock her and change the subject in a way that I can see hurts and frustrates her.

Day 3

Today you'll be understanding how you've been naturally leaning toward unassertive behavior in your responses. Again, today you are focusing on past behavior, but this is not to put you off. You will have the chance to put your mistakes right tomorrow.

Write a script of how you responded to the scenarios you wrote in Days 1 and 2. Write the words you said, and if you want, you can add how you felt and how you think the other person was affected. See if you can notice patterns.

For example, you might pick scenario 5 from your list:

"What is this, Jerry Springer? Why do you always want to talk about everything? You're so nosey I'm surprised you can hold your head up."

Think of other scenarios that are likely to arise, such as an unwanted guest inviting themselves over, and write the script of how you would likely respond:

"Yeah, of course you can come over. It's fine."

Observe how you feel when you write these responses and look out for the negative emotions like dread, resentment, and helplessness. You can write as many of these as you want, and they can be any length.

Day 4

Today you will write a script of the type of response you know would be healthy and assertive in your scenarios. Consider what an assertive person would say and write out the responses you think they will give. Again, write as many as you want of any length.

For scenario 5:

"I find it difficult to talk about that at the moment. I appreciate that you're being a good friend, but I'm just not ready. I really enjoy us just hanging out and taking my mind off things. I do want to talk about it all soon, when I feel ready."

Day 5

Now that you know how an assertive person would respond compared to what you've actually done in the past, you may have noticed key words or phrases that you either regret using or wish you had used. Write a list of what you should avoid using from your internal dialogue or with other people. This will help you to begin monitoring your vocabulary.

For example:

I don't mind.

Whatever you want to do is fine.

I don't deserve it anyway.

Who cares what I want.

Day 6

Words are important and powerful tools that help shape the world we live in. Agreeable people often find themselves using loaded language that prioritizes others over themselves. Write down some of examples of when you have used words that you didn't mean and consider what impression they give to other people.

For example:

Saying sorry when someone spills their drink on your work—this implies they are worth more than you and you are a pushover.

Saying "It was nothing, forget it," when someone thanks for doing them a big favor— this doesn't allow you to get the credit you deserve.

Then write out what you could say instead that accurately reflects the situation. For example:

"Excuse me, your drink's gone onto my stuff—do you mind cleaning that up please?"

"You're welcome."

Day 7

You now understand situations that have caused you to be unassertive, the correct ways to handle these types of scenarios, vocabulary to avoid, and the healthy language you can use instead. Today, be mindful of how you behave and think back to your scripts and chosen vocabulary if a moment arises where you might have been unassertive in the past. At the end of the day, write down what you are most proud of.

Phase 2

This second phase is about practicing your assertiveness outside of your comfort zone in a real-life setting and pushing your boundaries to build your confidence.

Day 9

Real life isn't like the fantasies we play out in our head. Today you'll be role-playing an extremely difficult situation to stop fear preventing you from trying even the smallest act of assertiveness. The role-play involves you being bullied by someone who wants you to do something you don't want to do and who won't give in. Your task is to deflect their anger while remaining in the assertive communication style and not submitting. You can ask someone you trust to play the part of the angry person or you can play both parts, imagining the kind of angry words that usually manipulate you.

Day 10

Today's tough role-play involves someone who will not take no for an answer. Your task is to remain assertive while forced into the role of broken record: continue repeating yourself and don't get angry or give in. Again, it is up to you whether you do this alone or with someone else.

Day 11

This challenging role-play is difficult for people-pleasers and those with low self-esteem because it focuses on resisting the urge to justify yourself and eventually talk yourself out of your own reasoning. Alone or with a friend, you are going to practice saying no in the shortest sentence possible. After a few practices, you should be able to keep your cool and go from "I really wish I could but it's just I'm going to be away that day, and you know I'd normally help you but . . ." to "No, I can't."

For the next two days, you will be practicing making small requests or imposing yourself on others in order to show yourself that you have as much right as anyone to do this and the consequences are nothing like the worst-case scenarios you've been picturing.

Some people find they're more confident with people they know very little or not at all, whereas others are terrified of the idea of talking to someone they haven't known for most of their life. Depending on where you stand, you can rearrange the order of Days 12 and 13 to ensure you do the easiest one for you first. This will grow your confidence for the next task.

Day 12

This is about practicing your assertiveness muscle in small ways. Remember that this is supposed to be fun, and rather than feeling nervous, think of it as anticipation and excitement. Enjoy the experience, blush, giggle, run away, feel embarrassed, but focus on how it really actually isn't that bad. You'll notice that most people will be happy to oblige if you are behaving assertively.

In a safe setting, such as a shop or a library, try the following:

Asking for the time.

Asking for directions.

Asking to have a photo with an individual or group.

Asking for a small loan that you'll pay back when your other friend arrives—for example, you're $5.00 short for a sandwich and you're starving.

Ask to use or borrow something of theirs.

Ask if you can keep something.

Day 13

You may have some friends who are highly demanding of you or it may just be that you've never had the courage to ask any of them to do something for you. Established relationships can be hard to change, and these friends may have become used to or even dependent on your lack of assertiveness. Despite this, people who truly care about you will welcome positive change and adapt to your assertive behavior. Today you'll be asking your friends for things. For example:

Asking them to bring you food.

Asking to borrow their favorite gadget.

Asking for something from your real life that you have been putting off.

Day 14

You've reached the halfway mark and it's time to look back at how far you've come, from the person on Day 1 facing their unassertive behavior to the confident communicator asserting themselves with strangers and friends. Write down what you have learnt, what surprised you the most, and what has made you the proudest of yourself so far.

Phase 3

This phase escalates you to higher degrees of assertiveness and involves manageable mini confrontations.

Day 15

If you used to be agreeable, accommodating, and a people-pleaser, you are likely in the habit of agreeing mindlessly with anyone, particularly acquaintances or strangers. Being contrarian is useful practice for someone who's usually submissive, so your task is to take every interaction with a stranger as an opportunity to break your habit of agreeing.

If someone in the queue behind you tells you they should open more checkouts, instead of agreeing, say, "They would lose money if they bought in more staff just for this half hour rush at lunchtime." Whatever it is they say, be contrarian in your response. You aren't being rude; just offer a different viewpoint that doesn't agree with what they just said.

Day 16

You're unlikely to break the habit of being agreeable in a day, so repeat the exercises from Day 15. Make a note of the fun you can have being contrary and whether with some people you broke down and agreed anyway.

Day 17

Your goal is to get your own way on something or to convince someone of something you choose. You're still being contrary and these mini confrontations are harmless demonstrations, so use your ever-rising confidence for today's task. For example:

Asking for an extra item on a set price menu dish.

Asking to swap seats with someone.

Asking someone if they know what time somewhere closes and then arguing that it closes an hour later.

Look out for the funniest reaction to write down at the end of the day.

Day 18

You're ready now to begin systematic desensitization by exposing yourself even more to the tasks you struggled with the most. You've shown yourself to be much more capable than you would have believed on Day 1, which is proof you can master more. Keep increasing the level of your mini confrontations: make more and more outlandish requests and practice role-plays where the person you're up against is insanely aggressive, someone you would never have dreamt of asserting yourself to before.

Day 19

Exposure therapy is based on the principle of respondent conditioning, where dogs who were fed when a bell was rung learned to salivate in anticipation at the sound of the bell despite no food appearing.

There are three type of exposure therapies, and today you will practice "in vitro," which is in real life. It's time to do what you have feared the most. Book a meeting with your boss and discuss a pay rise or have that conversation you've been dreading with your friend. Write down the relief you feel once it's out in the open.

Day 20

The second type of exposure therapy is imaginal. Today your task is to imagine yourself behaving assertively in your nightmare scenarios. You might want to try reimagining a situation where you were unassertive and that scarred you and picture yourself behaving in an assertive way. Write down how good it feels once you have confronted your fears in your mind.

Day 21

The third type of exposure therapy is introspective, where you confront your fear of bodily reactions such as a racing heart or shaking when nervous. Speak up in a meeting despite your pounding heart, and afterward ask someone for their feedback. Realizing they didn't even notice the physical effects you were ashamed of will give you confidence.

Phase 4

With all the progress you've made, it's now time to begin designing your life around being assertive, meeting your own needs, and prioritizing yourself over others.

Day 22

Write a detailed list of your needs and create an action plan of how you can achieve them. Understanding what you want will help you create the future you want. You could start with looking at things like job security, somewhere to live in a nice neighborhood, or furthering your education. Plan out how you can achieve this, whether by self-study or saving money every month.

Day 23

Now you understand your needs, you can begin to prioritize them. In order to have more time for yourself in the long term, use your judgement and cut out obligations to other people that you can reasonably remove. For example:

Stop letting my sister borrow my laptop all the time instead of buying her own.

Day 24

The remainder of Phase 4 is going to be you experiencing an obligation-free life, where you simply don't do something if you don't want to. You can choose to do this for a month for a more immersive experience.

You're going to say no to everything and fill your time with exactly what you want to do.

Make a list of events that you no longer have to go to, for example:

Work drinks when you're exhausted after a long week on Friday afternoons.

Your friend's party where there's always so many people there she ignores you.

Day 25

Write down the other obligations you are going to remove from your life, focusing on activities and duties. For example:

Putting the cups of everyone at work in the dishwasher at the end of the day when you do your own.

Doing volunteer training at work that no one else wants to do.

Day 26

Focus on the people you won't be obligated to while you're "off the grid." Think about people's behaviors and decide whether they're toxic takers, toxic nice people, aggressive, or users. Promise yourself you'll say no to everything they ask for the rest of this experience.

Day 27

Read back over your notes from the assertiveness action plan so far and contemplate what you've learnt. Continue to add obligations you now don't have to your list whenever you think of more and appreciate how freedom feels.

Day 28

Using yesterday's reflections, begin to set your new boundaries in stone. Pay attention to the relief you felt when you removed certain people or things. Consider if it's necessary to let them back into your life. You may continue with the obligation-free lifestyle for a few more weeks or you might be ready to add the important things back in.

Ensure you're not letting any obligations back into your life because you feel you "should." Prioritize yourself as you make these decisions because you are the one who matters the most and everything else comes second after you. You should have a list now of your needs, how you're going to achieve them, and the boundaries for your new assertive life that you refuse to compromise.

The assertiveness action plan is a guide and you can repeat days as often as you need until you feel fully confident. If you struggle with any particular area, refer to the relevant sections in the book. Not trying your hardest or putting tasks off is a choice. Deciding to take the first step and commit the task for Day 1 is being assertive and a great place to begin your journey.

Summary Guide

Chapter 1. The Balance of Assertiveness

- Assertiveness requires a delicate balance, especially if you are new to it. You may have started as too passive, but take care to not swing into the aggressive territory where you are robbing other people of their assertiveness. Aggressiveness does pay off in small ways, but there is often a long-term toll to pay.

- Tony Robbins succinctly articulated the six needs of human happiness you are likely keeping yourself from as a result of lacking assertiveness. They are **certainty**, **variety**,

significance, **love and connection**, **growth**, and **contribution**.

Chapter 2. "Just Let It Go."

- Too often, we feel like we must "let things go" for one reason or another. Are these reasons real or imagined? Important or irrelevant? Sometimes they appear important because of emotional blackmail, which is when there is an implicit threat that causes people to not assert themselves. There are four specific types of emotional blackmail threats: punisher, self-punisher, sufferer, and tantalizer.

- Even if there don't appear to be forms of emotional blackmail, the elements of FOG—fear, obligation, and guilt—will make you avoid speaking up.

- Other causes for "letting it go" include perfectionism and low self-esteem. The best way to learn to assert, as uncomfortable as it sounds, is consistent action and practice. Take baby steps at first, and the tension will begin to subside each time. You can find more about this in the assertiveness action plan in Chapter 9.

Chapter 3. Nobody Else Will Put You First

- Nobody else in your life will ever put you first, at least not in the way you deserve to be. This starts with self-prioritization. Altruism is an admirable trait, but only in balance can you be assertive for yourself.
- Self-compassion is where you put your own feelings and thoughts before those of others—for example, your happiness over the annoyance or disappointment of others.
- Self-acceptance is the knowledge that you are good enough, deserving, and worthy of your own needs. How can you ever assert yourself if you don't feel like you're good enough? You might just feel like you deserve nothing.
- Write the personal bill of rights down and post it on a wall in your room. These are rights, not privileges or luxuries. It's easy to forget until someone snaps you out of it.

Chapter 4. How to Ask for What You Want and Get It

- How do you ask for what you want? Well, you already know how. But we don't for various reasons, the first of which is that they should have known. They should have been able to read our minds and understand and anticipate our needs. Yes, in fairy tales, but not in reality.

- We also wait for people to take action because of the symbolic value we assign to things. We believe other people's symbolic value matches ours, which should inform their actions. But this is again projecting onto other people and depending on them to read our minds. We also can't subtly try to condition people into feeling the same symbolic value as us.

- Passive-aggressive behavior is concealed hostility masquerading as niceness, often with the goal of inducing some type of behavior. This happens when people are too angry to ask for what they want, typically.

- There are better and worse ways to making requests and asking for what you want. In fact, there are seven elements that will help you the most. Don't fill the silence after your ask, consider the other person's needs, make it easy and convenient, offer clear options, be direct and honest, be specific, and don't you dare pout if you get turned down.

Chapter 5. Saying N-O Without Tension

- Saying no is one of the toughest situations in everyday life because it is a mini confrontation every single time. But there are many ways to make this part of life smoother and less tense.
- Start saying "I don't" versus "I can't" because the former implies a policy, whereas the latter implies something to be negotiated. Likewise, get into the habit of saying no to specific and broad categories because that also implies a policy that you don't make exceptions for.
- It's important to also examine your beliefs surrounding no and what happens when

you agree or disagree. Importantly, you must think about how you maintain your personal space and balance the demands of other people. The cost-benefit analysis will come up very strongly in your favor.

- There are countless ways to say no. You already know a few, including the simplest way: "no" as a complete sentence. Understand that people will react strongly to you if you have a history of people-pleasing and being a doormat.

- Other methods of saying no include resisting the moment where you want to insert an addendum or caveat, creating hoops for people to jump through and themselves say yes to, baiting and switching with related or unrelated tasks, keeping it nonpersonal and focused on the specific circumstance, and passing the buck to someone who appears to be able to solve the problem at hand much better than you.

Chapter 6. The Need to Please

4. We tend to think being agreeable and accommodating are positive traits. They are, but selectively so. Studies have shown that too much of either conveys a negative impression to others—precisely what you want to prevent by not asserting yourself. Thus, it seems to make more sense to assert yourself on a consistent basis and stop the need for people-pleasing.

5. Boundaries become important very quickly to enforce, both to assert your rights and to defend against those who would seek to take advantage of you. TTs are the epitome of those who would seek to take advantage of you, and they come in many forms of selfishness and non-reciprocation.

6. People-pleasing ends when you start to take control of difficult situations and, essentially, become comfortable with confrontation. This is dictated by your cutoff point, which is the point at which you must act.

Chapter 7. The Instinct to Apologize

- Apologizing is the opposite of assertiveness—at least when you do it out of instinct like many of us are prone to do. Over-apologizing, however, does give a peek into how you view yourself and the patterns you've been exposed to. We are all products of our past experiences, and many have told us that apologies and not making waves is the best way to get through life unscathed.

- Men and women have markedly different approaches to over-apologizing, just like how they tend to be different in terms of assertiveness. It is mostly socialization and gender roles.

- Another reason for the instinct to apologize is to avoid conflict. Conflict is tense and uncomfortable, but it is the essence of assertiveness. Becoming comfortable with it by changing your vocabulary to apologize less is an important step.

- How do you apologize when you actually should? Include one of six elements articulated by Beth Polin and make sure to actually take responsibility and not deflect or blame others.

Chapter 8. Understanding Your Patterns

- There are generally four styles of communication: passive, aggressive, passive-aggressive, and assertive. You can guess which one is the best to shoot for.

- Assertive communication is standing up for yourself, being clear and direct when sharing your thoughts and feelings, and protecting your rights without taking away the rights of other people. Assertive communication is a product of high self-esteem and doesn't come naturally to people who haven't been taught to respect themselves and others and to value themselves on a physical, spiritual, and emotional level.